Pronounced "MY-dahn,"
"MAY-dahn," or "MI-dan," this word has
roots in a number of languages. It's been crossing
borders for generations from Tangier to Tehran, Batumi to Beirut.
It means "gathering place" or "square," often in the middle of
a city. The word originates in Arabic but translates to Hindi,
Urdu, Persian, Ukrainian, and even Latin. It's one
of the many ways we can see differences,
but in the end we're all the same.

MAYDĀN

RECIPES FROM LEBANON AND BEYOND

ROSE PREVITE WITH MARAH STETS

PHOTOGRAPHY BY JENNIFER CHASE

ABRAMS, NEW YORK

Contents

Left: Fattoush, Summer Salad with
Crisped Flatbread (page 78)

Introduction

I first heard the word in Ukraine: "Everyone is meeting at maydān." And then I kept hearing it: "The festival is at maydān." "The memorial is being held at maydān." "The revolution is happening at maydān."

Pronounced "MY-dahn," "MAY-dahn," or "MI-dan," the word is used throughout the Eastern Mediterranean, Central and South Asia, the Caucasus, Eastern Europe, and North Africa. It means the same thing everywhere: a central public meeting place, often in the middle of a city. A space for people to come together as a community to celebrate, to mourn, to rebel. That the word and ritual of the maydān have traveled so widely is a marvel. It shows, among other things, that maydān doesn't carry a passport, because moving between and among all those different places is not so easy if you're constrained by man-made borders.

Maydān isn't the only cross-lingual traveler in this region. The foodways also stretch across and through Morocco and Tunisia in the west, moving east through Lebanon, Syria, and Turkey up to Georgia, and as far east as Iran. Even if similar dishes don't have the same name everywhere or are made a bit differently from village to city to country, many of the ingredients and recipes from this part of the world have crossed borders, carried on the backs and in the minds of people who are sometimes making the journey willingly, and often not. Westerners associate many of these countries with tragedy and danger. Americans hear "Lebanon" and think of explosions and terrorists, Turkey brings a devastating earthquake to mind, and "Syrian civil war" rolls off the tongue more easily than the name of the country alone. Reporters perpetually seem able to find "conflict kitchen" stories in these neighborhoods. When we consider how and why this food has traveled so far, it's absolutely true that wrenching stories of forced migrations, famine, and war must be told, and heard.

Left: Enjoying the sunrise in Lebanon

But there are also other narratives to tell, and I have lived one of those.

The Inherited Immigrant Experience

I come from people who know very well what it means to feel extraordinarily proud of our culture while simultaneously softening the edges that might make our differences too noticeable. I was born and grew up in Ada, a tiny cornfield town in Ohio, the daughter of a Sicilian-American dad from New Jersey and a Lebanese-American mom straight out of Detroit. She and Dad saw how easy it was to lose those threads that tied us back to Lebanon, to Sicily; to assimilate so completely that you'd forget who your people were and where they came from.

I am obviously not an immigrant, but the inherited immigrant experience shaped my parents and me in turn. The unspoken rules about what you do inside your house that you can't do outside are passed down like a book of secret codes from one generation to the next.

All four of my great-grandparents on my mother's side came to this country from Lebanon between 1900 and 1908 and eventually settled in Detroit. Even though my grandparents, the next generation, had both grown up speaking Arabic, they did not teach the language to my mom and her siblings. But the food proved to be more resilient. My mother grew up only eating and cooking Lebanese food. And then I had a very similar experience.

Below: Baking man'ouche with Aunt Jan and Mom

Right: Kherbet Khanafar, my ancestral village in Lebanon

6

Lebanese in the Cornfields

I was a kid in the 1980s and early 1990s, before the Food Network became a 24/7 stream of boisterous dispatches from across the vibrant cultural melting pot that is America. For all I knew the people in my house and my cousins in Toledo were the only Lebanese in Ohio. Mom's perspective was that for us to identify with our culture we had to know it; and for us to love our culture, we had to show it. She was certain that by sharing the foods and flavors of our roots with as many people as possible, she'd charm them into understanding and accepting us, while simultaneously teaching my three brothers and me everything she wanted us to know and love about our heritage. Mom cooked every single night, and one and all were welcomed to our dinner table. My parents firmly believed that everything that happened at that table was important, and everything important happened at that table, while we prepared and ate platters full of home-cooked Lebanese and Italian food. This is all well and good—and maybe even a bit noble, in theory—but things are a little tougher out there when yours is the only locker at school that smells strongly of garlic. Of course, there are so many stories like mine, and really I was so fortunate as I enjoyed growing up in Ohio and didn't get overtly bullied. But, sure, people said some weird stuff, and I was asked "So what are you?" all the time.

And there was a standard of beauty in Ohio that was not my family's kind of beauty. It was about light hair and light eyes and a breezy comfort hanging out with the boys after the football games. My dad was the faculty advisor to Ohio Northern University's International Student Association, for students from abroad; every year I looked forward to the fashion show the students put on to show off the styles of dress from their home countries. I remember so clearly the young women from Lebanon and Jordan, with long dark hair and brown eyes like mine, who walked the "runway" dressed in silky fabrics dyed in rich jewel tones and whose gold bangle bracelets sparkled in the light and jangled together as if dancing and singing. I recognized beauty in them—in their faces, in how they dressed, and in the way they carried themselves. What they had felt familiar and certainly much closer to me than anything at school or at the mall. Through them I connected to a place where I eventually arrived.

Top left: Eating grape leaves at a young age

Bottom left: Making tabouleh for the masses

Above top: Aunt Joan and Aunt Jan visiting the homeland for the first time

Above bottom: Cooking with cousins in Bishmizzine, Lebanon, my maternal grandfather's village

From as far back as I can remember, I carried with me a palpable sense of being different, an "other." There's no question that this was partly because of how conservative and strict my parents were, especially Dad. I wasn't allowed to go to slumber parties. We didn't trick-or-treat on Halloween. Dating was out of the question until I was just a few months away from leaving for college. Needless to say, I didn't have a normal social life by the standards of most of the kids I grew up with, or really of anyone that I've met—even in my adult life. And naturally our food was also outside the norm. All I wanted to bring to school for lunch was a peanut butter and grape jelly sandwich on store-bought white bread and to have parties like my friends did, with pizza and Mountain Dew. Instead, my lunch was a pita stuffed with lamb in lemony tahina, and when my friends came over, Mom served them skewers of grilled chicken with bowls of garlicky toum sauce.

So we were that weird family in our homogenous, not ethnically diverse town, and it was definitely rough for a while. But by the time I was in high school, the kids knew that ours was the house to come to for great food; and their parents had figured it out, too. Mom began catering out of our tiny home kitchen, as well as doing Lebanese cooking demos at the Hardin County Fair. Meanwhile Dad's one and only hobby outside of his work as a professor of pharmaceutical law at Ohio Northern University (ONU) was making and selling street food. His own father, Al, whose family lived and worked in a Pennsylvania coal-mining town and who didn't go past the eighth grade, had grown up to own and run an Italian grocery store and butcher shop in New Jersey. Pop (that's what we called him) lived above and then alongside the shop, which is where my dad grew up. Dad was the first in his family to go to college, so he never considered taking over the family business. But his passion for food drove him to wake up us four kids early every Saturday morning to help him make mountains of Italian sausage and then spend Sunday at local fairs and festivals selling them in sandwiches. My parents were not professional cooks, but they did buy all their pots and pans at restaurant supply stores, which wasn't commonplace in those days, especially in rural Ohio. And they taught me at a very early age how to whip up batches of tabbouleh for three hundred and enough Italian sausage to feed both a small army and the opposing side.

Those were the ordinary days. And then there were the special ones. For holidays (see page 116), weddings, or any other cause for group celebration (or mourning), we'd drive up to my mom's family in Detroit days before the event itself, or my aunts and their husbands and kids would descend on our house. For a full day or two, my mom and aunties formed assembly lines in the kitchen and dining room to prepare all the components of the feasts. Each aunt (and, when we got older, the cousins) had an assigned job for every dish, whether grinding fresh lamb for kibbeh, chopping walnuts for baklawa, mixing fatayer dough, filling and rolling grape leaves, dipping warm sambousek into sugar syrup laced with orange blossom water, or any of what seemed like dozens of other tasks. The house smelled incredible from almost the moment they arrived, and the women's voices—often bickering, and often laughing—were like a well-worn coat I would put on and be surrounded by the commingling aromas and music of their togetherness.

New Frontiers

Yet in spite of all of the focus on food in my house, until I went to college, I didn't really eat at restaurants other than the casual Italian spots near where my dad's family lived in New Jersey. I'd never had (or seen) okra, or truly fresh fish. We were Midwestern Middle Easterners. My first trip outside of the United States, for a college semester abroad in Granada, Spain, showed me that delicious food existed outside the walls of families' homes and persuaded me that international travel was going to be a very important, even necessary, part of my life. I'd never been on my own before. I fell in love with a guy named Carlos, and I took a siesta every day at three o'clock so that I'd be ready to go out until long after dark. On those nights out in Granada—one of the most fun cities in the world for a college kid, in my opinion—everyone danced and drank on the streets until very late. Old, young, it didn't matter. They really taught me to love life.

And the patatas bravas! Many nights we would buy paper cups full of these hot, crispy little chunks of perfectly fried potatoes to eat on the way home. It was the first time food that wasn't prepared by my family meant something special to me. From then on, I could connect everywhere I'd been to something I ate while there, and that ingredient or dish forever after reminded me of a specific place, person, or sometimes even a moment from a trip. To this day patatas bravas symbolize my first taste of freedom.

What I didn't—couldn't—know at the time was that this love for travel and food memories would someday lead me to be slumped on a Trans-Siberian Railway train ten thousand miles from home, watching through the smudged window as one snow-and-soot-covered village after another wove in and out of focus, wondering gloomily what the hell I was doing there. If you'd asked me on one of those nights in Granada where I'd be in a decade or so, I would never in a million years have guessed that I'd be sitting on a shabby train car, feeling very empty. Nothing about most of my thirty-something years of life up until then hinted that anything about my current situation was likely.

After graduating from college in the early 2000s, I moved to Washington, DC, where I soon began to pursue my master's degree in public policy. I was preparing to help save the world. In the meantime I still had to eat, so between classes and interning at Human Rights Watch, I waited tables and slung cocktails at a bar in Southeast DC. One of my regular customers was a reporter for the *Baltimore Sun* named David Greene. We hit it off so well that we got engaged a few years later in Istanbul and then we ate delectable fish sandwiches (page 219) in celebration.

Left: Visiting Muscat, Oman

To Russia, in Love

Soon after David and I were married in 2007, we moved from DC to New York City, where I worked for the city council and David for NPR. And then David got the assignment of his dreams: foreign correspondent, based in Moscow. David would want me to clarify that it was only the first part he'd been hoping for; the precise base of operations was not spelled out. In retrospect, his dreams should probably have been more specific. I spoke not one word of the language—to this day I have what I call taxicab Russian. No matter! My semester in Granada had convinced me that I was extremely international and could assimilate anywhere. I assumed I'd find something to do once I'd learned a bit of Russian; I could always wait tables or tend bar, as I'd done throughout college and grad school. Except Moscow is a lot different than Granada, or Turkey, or anywhere else I'd been until then—or since. It turned out that I wasn't actually allowed to work in Russia, an important detail that only became fully clear to me once I was on the ground there.

So, after years of hustling my butt off to learn and do everything I could to get where I wanted to be professionally (helping to save the world, you may recall), I was suddenly effectively holding still, which I have never been terribly good at, and living in a challenging and frigid foreign city (you may also recall that I have Mediterranean blood). There were some dark days, like the late afternoon when I caught sight of a reflection in the darkened windows of the kitchen (it was only 4:00 P.M. and already pitch black outside) and what I saw was a woman with her hand up the butt of a half-thawed chicken and the phone crammed between ear and shoulder while she waited for her husband to answer and let her know what time he would be able to leave work and come home for dinner. What I saw was familiar, for I'd seen my own mother in exactly the same pose, making exactly the same call, hundreds of times in my childhood. I googled myself and the only results were our wedding announcement; I googled David and there were links to the many stories he'd been posting for NPR. I often found myself reckoning with the uncomfortable notion that I had become a thirty-something housewife without having planned it, and at the expense of my own personhood.

It absolutely wasn't all bad. In fact, perhaps my most enduring love affair—with the food and culture of the country of Georgia—was sparked on one of our very first nights in Moscow. In the "Sad Sam" building in Moscow where many foreign journalists live, we hosted a dinner for some of the other reporters. We'd enlisted the help of a Georgian woman to cook the meal, and the first thing I saw her do was chop an enormous pile of walnuts in our tiny kitchen. I mean, so very many walnuts! My mind went immediately back to my twelve-year-old self standing at our dining room table surrounded by my mom and aunts while we rolled, stuffed, and folded scores of sambousek (page 254) for Christmas. Every dish the lovely cook prepared that night—rolled eggplant stuffed with chopped walnuts, lamb and tarragon stew, chicken in walnut sauce—was completely new yet somehow familiar to me, and all of it smelled and tasted amazing. I was in love.

Top and right: Drinking tea at a roadside restaurant in Oman with David

Though that was my very first taste of authentic Georgian food, I had plenty of opportunity after that night to experience more. When we lived in Russia, the ruble was doing great against the dollar. It was the heyday of the billionaire oligarch, and the restaurant scene in Moscow was on the uptick. The most popular places served extremely expensive Italian and French food. The only restaurants that served consistently great, affordable food were Georgian. Thankfully there were a lot of these.

Most of our culinary discoveries happened thanks to David's frequent assignments abroad. We visited more than thirty countries during our three years in Russia, and we ate incredible food in so many of them. Eventually we even got to see the quiet villages and stunningly beautiful mountains of Georgia for ourselves. I was overwhelmed by the Georgian people's kindness, hospitality, and oh my goodness, the food. We ate exceedingly well, enjoying many of the dishes you'll see on page 165.

The Train to Everywhere

Then, toward the end of David's stint in Russia, he and his producer arranged the ne plus ultra of reporting assignments: riding the full route of the Trans-Siberian Railway, from Moscow to its terminus nearly six thousand miles away, Vladivostok, a port city in the southeasternmost part of Russia. Naturally I accompanied them. In December 2011 we embarked on the adventure, and our food experiences over the three-and-a-half weeks ranged from the sublime to the ridiculous. The sublime came roughly at the point where the train crossed onto the Asian continent, and we left European Russia behind. The dividing line is the Ural Mountains, and situated in the foothills of these mountains is the city of Yekaterinburg, where the Romanovs—Tsar Nicholas II and his family—were executed by the Bolsheviks in July 1918, and where our train stopped on a very cold day. We spent little time in the city itself, instead driving about forty minutes out of town to Sagra, a little village of fewer than one hundred tiny wooden houses heated only by small stoves.

Two different families had invited us to visit them in their homes, and they set out feasts of tea and cakes and pickles. Viktor, the charming, bearded patriarch of the village, lived in the first home we visited. Viktor sweetly took it upon himself to rid me of the brutal head cold I'd picked up. His homespun remedy was a generous shot of vodka enhanced with an eye-popping amount of freshly ground black pepper. I had to take my medicine—there was simply no getting around it. To Viktor's credit, he prepared the same shot for himself, presumably as a preventative measure against catching my cold. The extremely spicy shot was followed by a pickled tomato. Neither helped my burning throat, but my head did clear up for a good thirty minutes and for that I was very grateful. On the other hand, kindly Viktor's home didn't have indoor plumbing. We never knew what we'd find in the rural parts of Russia when it came to toilets. Lots of people still use outhouses. They are brave souls; it never got above 0 degrees Fahrenheit (minus 18 degrees Celsius) while I was there.

The second house we visited was owned by Andrei and his wife, Oxana. Andrei loved to hunt, as evidenced by the large number of guns lying around the house. Meanwhile his wife, Oxana, had only two gas burners to cook on and no kitchen sink. The only running water in the house was located in the bathroom. Oxana made the best eggplant spread I'd ever had—it struck me that were it served in a restaurant in Manhattan they'd call it "tapenade" and charge a fortune for it. Oxana had a collection of porcelain souvenirs from faraway places, which she proudly showed me one by one. They were all gifts—she hadn't been to any of those exotic places. But she did have an indoor toilet, which she was almost as happy about as I was.

And then there was the ridiculous, most of which we experienced while on the train itself, where the enticing idea of accompanying David to Siberia on the world's longest railway met up with the reality of said trip not too long after we reboarded the train in Yekaterinburg, somewhere just north of where Kazakhstan and Mongolia nearly meet. By this time, some of what we initially perceived as the charming quirks of foreign train travel—things like sleeping four to a cabin and no prohibition on passengers smoking anywhere, at any time—had become significantly more consequential in

Above: Russia

our day-to-day lives. For instance, in spite of an ornate dining car and a very long and detailed menu—whose front cover was adorned with the proclamation, "Dear visitors of the dining-car! Daily from 12-00 to 16-00 local time the dining-car gives complex dinners."—they served nothing but borscht. On the plus side it was delivered to our table by a short-tempered attendant who never troubled himself to hide his irritation when we tried to order anything on the menu that wasn't borscht. There were few other options. When the train pulled into a station, vendors on the platform sold kielbasa-type sausage, and we'd dash off just long enough to buy some and hop back on. Additionally, a very blonde, buxom woman clad in a black leather skirt and high heels sauntered the aisles selling cabbage-filled pies exclusively to male passengers, often while sitting on their laps. One of her customers told me her name was Natasha.

The greatest gastronomic gift the porters gave us was unreserved access to huge samovars full of piping hot water on every car. I ate my weight in ramen and drank so much tea that I was constantly in need of the less-than-amazing train bathrooms or village outhouses. No wonder I'd caught that cold! I wrote these words in my journal after one particularly long stretch with no stops:

> *Entering 58th hour on the train with no breaks. Going to lose my mind. Have serious cabin fever. Must get off the train. The food car workers have become our sworn enemies. We are existing on cups of instant noodles, bread, cheese, instant oatmeal, and granola bars. I want a veggie stir fry very badly.*

Thus was my state of mind that day. I sat slumped and a bit cold, staring out the train window, and wondering not only what the hell I was doing there, but what the hell I was doing, period. I had now spent three years in Moscow with (and often without) David; more of our marriage had happened in Russia than out of it. We were heading back to the U.S. in the next calendar year, specifically to DC, where David had been promoted to an anchor seat on NPR's *Morning Edition*. And I was . . . what, exactly?

Three and a half weeks traveling across Siberia on a sometimes very slow train can warp your sense of where in the world you are, and where in the world you belong. In this mood it became easier for me to adopt the fatalistic attitude that I'd been observing from afar the past few years. Our Russian friends loved to remind me and anyone within earshot that since we could easily die tomorrow, we might as well do whatever we have in mind today. I pondered my mortality and thought hard about what made me happy. I recalled the hours-long Georgian supras where strangers become friends (see page 164), and I thought about Oxana, Andrei, and Viktor and how enthusiastically they'd welcomed and fed us. I considered all the hospitality I had experienced during our travels, in so many different languages, and how it had made me feel content and at peace. It dawned on me that what I loved most of all was the food at the center of all that warmth and generosity. I allowed myself to realize that I'd always loved working with food. I'd worked hard in bars and restaurants during school, but I had never considered a career in food. I had been afraid to commit to it in that way—especially after getting a graduate degree in public policy. I believed that going all-in on working with food might be something I'd do later in life, like my mom did when she finally got her own brick-and-mortar restaurant at the age of sixty, after the kids were all out of the house.

On that train I came to accept that "later" was now. Making food, serving food, making people feel at home, comfortable and cared for—that was my dream assignment. I'd never felt more viscerally that if I were going to fail, so be it. The seeds were planted; there would be no more waiting. When we got back home, I was going to open a restaurant.

David likes to say that my restaurants wouldn't exist if I hadn't been so cold in Russia.

Lighting the Fire at Maydān

Left: Learning the ancient way of grinding grain into flour, Oman

Above: Opening Maydān's iconic blue door

I returned to the U.S. with a sense of purpose I hadn't felt in a long time and all the fire and drive of the newly converted. I intended to wring every single good thing from my travels and my upbringing to give to my guests. In 2014 I opened my first restaurant, Compass Rose, in Washington, DC, with a menu of street foods from around the world. I love that I can look at an item on the menu even today and a flood of warmth comes over me as I remember those places, people, or moments I will forever associate with that dish. To my surprise and enduring delight, we were enthusiastically embraced by the people of, in, and around DC. Before long I knew that I'd found my calling, and that it was already ringing for me to add to the family.

I didn't have to think too hard about what would be next. I had wanted a fire-fueled restaurant ever since the city hadn't allowed us to install the outdoor kitchen I wanted as part of the street food concept at Compass Rose. I went on a mission to find a location where I could cook food the way street food vendors all over the world cook. When I further decided I wanted to pay tribute to the women who taught me how to cook and about hospitality, the food I grew up with made the most sense. Since the region my family comes from is incredibly ancient, it seemed logical to use the most traditional form of cooking food—live fire—as a way to honor it.

So I would explore and expand outward from my Lebanese roots and the food of my soul and we would cook this food on fire. On-the-ground research was the only way to make it happen. The kind of food I wanted on our menu had to be experienced in person and on the spot. As my chefs and I planned our summer 2017 trip through Morocco, Tunisia, Lebanon, Turkey, and Georgia, I knew that it wasn't going to be enough to go to big cities or even medium towns and talk to chefs and other food professionals. We couldn't find the recipes or techniques in books or online for the kind of food we wanted because that sort of record-keeping of home cooking in these places simply didn't exist. So we set out on what we called the "cooking with grandmas" tour, searching for foods, spices, and recipes we could replicate back home. We were welcomed into strangers' homes with open arms, and we left friends. The women we met and talked to reminded me of my mom and my aunts. I felt a kinship with them as I listened to their stories about keeping their traditions. I reached a new level of understanding and gratitude toward my mom for her insistence that I had to know and love the culture and foods of my roots.

And our suspicions about the need for this level of hands-on research were confirmed when one of our teachers, a woman in Tunisia, told us, "You can't find authentic Tunisian food in the restaurants. Men work in the restaurants. You have to come into our homes where the women are." Exactly so. On this trip we let the universe lead us and we found absolutely wonderful people who taught us magical things. We saw parts of the world that are more beautiful than anything we'd ever seen. And we connected with people despite language limitations, understanding one another through the most human things we all share. We saw that our differences really aren't so many after all, especially when it comes to food, which simply doesn't recognize the borders drawn by men.

That cross-cultural connection resonates like the hum of a communal meeting spot where strangers can gather, and so we opened Maydān in DC in 2017, with dishes drawn from my Lebanese roots and our travels through and extensive research about the region from Morocco and Tunisia in the west; moving east across North Africa through Egypt, Lebanon, Syria, and Turkey; then north up to Georgia and the Caucasus; south to Yemen and Oman; and as far east as Iran. (Though I've never been able to visit Iran in person, I am lucky to have Iranian friends who are generous with their recipes for authentic dishes from their country of origin.) And again we were thrilled that the city, and indeed the whole country, responded so positively to us. Named one of both *Food & Wine* and *Bon Appétit*'s best restaurants of the year in 2018, we also received our first Michelin star in 2020.

And, even as I write this book, I have a couple of other restaurant and food-service concepts in the works. First, in the Virginia-side suburbs of DC, we are opening the very first Kirby Club, which is my take on the Lebanese-American story. The menu there is made up of twists on a lot of what I ate growing up, using many of the ingredients in this book, but with more of an American feel. And in Los Angeles, I am working to open the food and retail marketplace of my dreams, inspired by the feel and content of outdoor markets in Fez and Marrakesh and the night markets in Southeast Asia.

A few years ago my mom found an article from 1998 that she had saved from our local paper, the *Ada Herald*. The article featured the two of us talking about turning her penchant for cooking into an official catering business. None of that journey was easy, which made it all the more inspiring. Mom taught me the importance of feeding people around a table. She and her mother, aunts, and sisters taught me that food can heal and that cooking is a way of showing love. Neither of my restaurants nor any of the other food and wine projects I'm involved with would ever have happened if they hadn't taught me those critical lessons. But if you had told us back in '98 that all that cooking together would end up turning into a Michelin-starred Middle Eastern restaurant in Washington, DC, Mom and I would have laughed and asked what Michelin was.

Left: Early evening at Maydān

Above: At Maydān's main bar

The Wine of Georgia and Lebanon

It might be a surprise to learn that Georgians make excellent wine and that they're so proud of it that sometimes when you pass through immigration, the officer at the airport will stamp your passport and hand it back to you along with a gift: a small bottle of local wine. They have good reasons for their pride. The country has several distinct microclimates allowing many different types of grapes to grow and wine to be made—as many as five hundred native grape varietals according to some estimates—and DNA tests have proven that wine has been made on their land for at least eight thousand years. But what really blows me away is that in many parts of the country, producers ferment, age, and store wine just as they did all those millennia ago: In large clay vessels called *qvevri*, which are buried in the ground and sealed with beeswax or clay to protect the precious liquid inside. Georgia has also been known longer than any other place for their amber wines, whose unique flavor, tannic mouthfeel, and beautiful orangey hue are produced by days or even months of "skin contact" between the pressed juice and the skins of the white wine grapes used to make the wine.

When we lived in Moscow, our expat friends sang the praises of Georgian winemakers and told us before our first trip to Georgia that their bottles were the best and most affordable. Unfortunately, they were also unavailable in Russia, since the Kremlin had imposed an embargo on them in 2006, ostensibly for quality issues but actually in response to Georgian protests against Russian influence. That embargo lasted for six years, by which time the world's wine market had changed dramatically, making it challenging if not impossible for Georgian producers to regain the market share in Russia they'd once had. As someone with a keen interest in foreign policy and social justice, it shocked me to learn the ways wine is geopolitical and to witness how a huge, powerful country could do so much damage to a smaller one with these tactics.

Once I learned this history and traveled more, I realized a lot of other places in the world face similar hurdles, including my ancestral homeland, Lebanon. Lebanese winemakers have been tending vines and pressing grapes and aging and bottling the juice for generations, but few people expect them to make the great wines that they do. Lebanon's wine making has a deep-rooted association with France, a by-product of the French occupation during the first half of the twentieth century. But while it's true that when France moved into Lebanon they brought many of their grapevines with them, the fact is that Lebanon was growing its own grapes and making its own wine long before the French arrived, and they've continued to do so and even expanded in the many decades since the French withdrew. Today, vineyards stretch across the Beqaa Valley and other deep valleys in Lebanon as well as up the sides of the roaring mountains that line those valleys. Growing here are grapes that are familiar to French wine enthusiasts such as cabernet and cabernet franc. A few well-known winemakers, especially Chateau Musar, which was founded during the French occupation, make really nice wines using primarily these grapes. They have done a lot to get Lebanon the attention it deserves, especially in the U.S. But there are also indigenous grapes, such as Merwah and Obaideh, and the real excitement and innovation is happening in the vineyards and cellars of much smaller producers (such as Mersel) across this tiny country that are trying to expose more people to these indigenous varietals.

Learning about the grapes and the people working so hard in these places led me to seek out as much wine from these countries as I could once I was back in the U.S. It's my personal Putin protest to sell as much Georgian wine at my restaurants as possible. And since those early days in Georgia, I've learned of other places where excellent wine is being made but very few people worldwide know about them. This is why David and I helped start Go There wines, an innovative production and distribution company. We focus on grapes and regions that have not been explored by Americans, and we partner with people in those places who are pushing the boundaries and challenging the conventions of their countries with their winemaking. Our partners are amazing people, like two sisters in Georgia, where the wine industry is dominated by men; a Syrian refugee living and making wine in exile in Lebanon; and a Black woman breaking both race and gender barriers in South Africa. Each has had unique challenges reaching a wider audience, but they wouldn't want you to buy their wine because of their struggles; they want you to buy it because it's great wine.

Top left: Eddie during harvest time, Lebanon

Bottom left: Trying new vintages out of the tanks, Lebanon

Below: Grape vineyards at Kefraya Winery

A NOTE ABOUT THE ORIGINS OF THE RECIPES IN THIS BOOK

My book shares its name with my restaurant, and though there is certainly some common purpose between the two, this is not a restaurant cookbook. I'm a Lebanese grandmother at heart, and the recipes here are the sort of warm, comforting, and delicious fare that grandmas all over the world are known for. This food is perfectly suited to the home cook because it doesn't all have to be ready at the same time, and everything on the table is meant to be shared. I use simple ingredients to make uncomplicated dishes—dips, spreads, kebabs, and stews—bursting with bright flavors. Similarly while individual countries might claim one dish or another as their own, I don't designate a single country for many of these recipes. When I present a dish made a certain way it's because that is how I learned how to do it growing up or during my travels. Naturally the dishes have been adapted to use ingredients that we can find readily in the U.S.; however, I don't whitewash or indiscriminately Americanize or put "fusion" spins on any of the dishes. The food is specific, but I have strived to also make it accessible. I want you to feel totally comfortable and inspired to discover a part of the world that might be unfamiliar to you. Also, if you're from a family with a background like mine, and you grew up eating lots of the same kinds of things, but no one wrote any of it down, I hope this reminds you of home, and maybe even gives you a starting place for recreating some of these dishes, just like you remember them. I hope with all of my heart that your kitchen will come alive with the aromas of these places—I invite you to visit with your eyes, nose, and taste buds what you perhaps have not yet experienced in person.

When an Arabic name for a recipe is offered here, it is either from my childhood or something I've learned from friends and distant family since becoming an adult. I don't speak Arabic, and I claim no expertise on the subject. Any time an English speaker writes an Arabic word using our alphabet, the best we can do is transliterate, or, as many of my friends say, "spell like it sounds to you."

A NOTE ABOUT THIS REGION OF THE WORLD

I can't share so much about the beauty that has been produced in this part of the world without also calling attention to how terrible the circumstances are for so many who live there. War, occupation, repression of human and especially women's rights, foreign interference, government corruption. This is hardly an exhaustive list of the existential challenges that face

many of these people every day and all put enormous, unfathomable pressure on regular people who want and deserve nothing more or less than any of us does—to live, work, and play in safety, to raise a family, to feed themselves and their loved ones nourishing food, to live without fear. As much as I hope to reach as many readers as possible with delectable recipes and beautiful photos and stories, I hope even more that these same readers will look at the part of the world where all of that greatness comes from with renewed empathy and compassion for the people who are behind all of it.

A NOTE ABOUT COVID

I conceived of this book long before the Covid-19 pandemic took over daily life in the United States beginning early in 2020. Yet I wrote the book during the pandemic, and that affected everything about my life, my restaurants, and yes, the book.

I'm struck by how interested people are in how it all went down. I'm asked constantly, "How bad was it?" "How did you do it?" "How did your restaurants survive?" The answers, in order, are horrible, by the skin of our teeth, and with grit, determination, and a major dose of luck.

I've built my life and businesses entirely by bringing people together. I long to celebrate with them and to comfort them. This is my superpower, and the most heartbreaking part was that at the height of the pandemic we couldn't bring people together. I'm not exaggerating when I say that for a good while I was frankly lost, adrift, and terrified. Then the people at the humanitarian organization, World Central Kitchen, called and asked if we would cook for the city.

When I was growing up the first thing we did when someone did anything—got sick, died, had something worth celebrating—was to cook and deliver food for them. And to be clear, this isn't in my memory just a Lebanese thing; it's also a midwestern thing. Food happened constantly. It seemed like everybody was always cooking something for somebody else. Or growing enough vegetables in their gardens for everybody else.

So yes, we told World Central Kitchen, of course, we will cook for the city. And it was such an enormous relief to get back to our purpose—back to what I was born to do. This has been an extraordinary time for all of us, individually and collectively. And while most of the recipes here have already been around long enough to have transcended many human events, we mere mortals are still reckoning with what this event means. I guess what I'm trying to say is that I'm grateful to be here, in this place, sharing this food, with you.

AND LASTLY, SOME COCKTAILS

If you're reading these words, it's likely fairly easy to believe that good food is important to me. But I was also a bartender for most of my adult life, and it's from this perspective that I make the following assertion. Good food is even better with a cocktail.

To underscore this point, and because like any good bartender I enjoy mixing things up (see what I did there?), I have included a cocktail at the end of chapters two through eight. These are all drinks that can certainly stand on their own, like any good cocktail should, but they also play very well with food, as all my favorite cocktails do. Any of these will make a meal more fun, and a dinner party even more more fun.

Left: Baking in Oman

Above: Making drinks at Maydān

Pantry Staples

There are a few items that I always have on hand, and if you have them, too, it'll make most recipes in this book no more challenging to shop for than whatever you can get with a quick stop at the grocery store.

DRIED MINT

A year-round staple in my family, no matter how much mint is growing fresh outside. Indeed, my grandmother, who we called Sitti, grew mint all over the yard of her house in Royal Oak, Michigan, where my aunt Jennifer now lives. During the summer the giant Ping-Pong table in the basement was draped in a big sheet whose every inch seemed to hold drying mint. After each harvest was sufficiently dried, it would be packaged up in dozens of plastic bags for distribution to family and friends, and as soon as one harvest was bagged, the next was already being laid out on the table. It was an every-day-in-summer affair, and that Ping-Pong table never saw the light of day between late spring and early fall. I'm still excited whenever Aunt Jen hands me a bag of mint dried from the garden—that's right, the Ping-Pong table still hasn't retired from drying Sitti's mint. On the occasions I need to actually buy it, I go to Lebanese, Persian, or Indian stores, where they sell very good quality dried mint in larger bags or cans.

BLUE FENUGREEK

I'd never heard of blue fenugreek before I encountered Georgian food, first in Moscow, and then in the country itself, and now I don't know what I would do without it. Unique to Georgia, where it is called utsho suneli, blue fenugreek is related to the Indian fenugreek more common here in the U.S., but it has a sweeter, warmer aroma and flavor. It's phenomenal on meat and in stews. It's easy to buy it online.

SUMAC

In the restaurants we use ground sumac liberally, sprinkling it over many dips and sauces, rubbing it on fish and meat, and seasoning fresh and cooked vegetables alike with it. Tart like fresh lemon, with a light sweetness and a deep and beautiful red color, ground sumac is kept in a shaker on my table right along with the salt and pepper so that I can add some punch to anything and everything.

SALTS

I may have grown up eating only the iodized table salt that my mom swears by to this day, but you wouldn't know it to look in my spice cabinet. Salt is one of my favorite things to buy wherever I travel. I regularly have no fewer than six different kinds of salt on hand and each of these is distinct for its grain or texture or flavor; among these I always have kosher, a premixed salt-and-za'atar mixture, and a delicate, flaky sea salt, such as Maldon or fleur de sel, for sprinkling on fresh food and finishing cooked dishes just before serving them. Beyond those essentials I love all kinds of salts mixed with herbs, spices, or other ingredients, such as chiles or peppercorns.

ORANGE BLOSSOM WATER AND ROSE WATER

These fragrant waters add floral aroma and flavor to desserts and drinks. My love for rose water, in particular, began when I was a kid. My paternal grandma, whose name was also Rose, grew beautiful roses at the New Jersey home she shared with my grandfather. Every summer we'd visit them, and it was there that my dad, the pharmacist, showed me how to extract and distill the essence of those roses into perfume and fragrant water. I love that memory, but there is definitely no need to learn how to make it yourself! These waters are readily available in Lebanese, Persian, and Indian stores and online. If you've never before used orange blossom and rose water in your cooking, I advise you to add only a portion of what is called for in recipes and taste as you go. As much as I personally adore orange blossom and rose waters, many don't, and that's just fine. Remember that you can always add more, but you can't take it out once it's in there.

POMEGRANATE MOLASSES

Made from pure pomegranate juice, pom molasses has become a kind of "secret" ingredient among American chefs, who have discovered what people in this region of the world have long known, and it's why it is drizzled over or poured into so many savory dishes. Each drop is a concentrated burst of earthy, sweet, tangy, and tannic flavor that elevates pretty much everything it touches. There are recipes for it online, but there's no need to make it as pomegranate molasses is readily available in many well-stocked grocery stores; Lebanese, Persian, and Indian stores; and online.

TAHINI

This creamy paste made from sesame seeds is ubiquitous in this part of the world and an essential ingredient in beloved dips like hummus and baba ghanoush. Though most mainstream supermarkets now carry some kind of tahini, and maybe even more than one kind, I urge you to seek out the Beirut brand, which packs tons of flavor into a paste that is remarkably easy to stir and pour and is available at Lebanese, Persian, and Indian grocery stores and online.

UNFILTERED LEBANESE EXTRA-VIRGIN OLIVE OIL

Lebanese olive oil is wildly underrated, in my opinion, and it's one of the reasons that the flavors at Maydān are so good. It's nutty and rich, and those qualities are especially present when the oil is not filtered. As with so many of my pantry items, this type of oil is available in Lebanese grocery stores and online. To ensure you get all the goodness, confirm that the oil is unfiltered before you buy it; this is not always indicated in the name of the product.

BEN'S ORIGINAL RICE (FORMERLY UNCLE BEN'S)

I grew up eating just this one kind of rice (and eating it many times a week, to be clear). Ben's rice is parboiled, or "converted," which means that it is steam cooked and then dried before packaging; this process helps prevent it from sticking or clumping during cooking. It also means that it requires more liquid and a little more time to cook than regular long-grain white rice. It has very little flavor of its own and I know it's not trendy and might even shock some of my chef friends, but I stand by this truth: Ben's Original rice always cooks perfectly, is always available at pretty much any grocery store I'm in, and I never use anything else for my family recipes. I don't know how or why my Lebanese family chose to build our culinary history on this particular rice, but I can say that the decision was made long before I was born, for my grandmother and her sisters also used it religiously. For more information on Egyptian rice, which I have learned to love almost as much as Ben's, see page 144.

GROUND LAMB IN MY FREEZER

This is one of my absolute staples, but for years I could never be sure if it would be stocked at the store or not. With each passing year it's wonderful to see how much more common good-quality lamb is in regular grocery stores. Still, though, it's expensive, so when it's on sale I buy a couple of extra pounds and throw them in my freezer. This is how I guarantee that my path to a delicious pot of koosa (page 102) or rice with lamb (page 144) is always smooth and easy. If ground lamb is hard to find where you are, ask the butcher to grind a leg of lamb for you, or bring it home to grind yourself.

LABNE

I keep a tub of labne in my fridge the way other people I know keep and use plain Greek or regular yogurt, or sour cream, or crème fraiche. It's an ingredient in many of the dishes I cook, but it doesn't need to be called for in the recipe to give a creamy, tangy boost to pretty much anything it touches—soups, stews, roasted vegetables, meats, fish, cake, pudding, fruit, you name it.

FRESH CHILES

Finally, I use a lot of fresh chiles like serranos, Fresnos, and habaneros in my recipes because I love the flavor and heat they bring to food. Sometimes I call for them to be seeded, sometimes not, but in any and all cases, you can decide whether to remove all, some, or none of the seeds and ribs, which is where most of the heat is found in chiles. We can't see capsaicin, the active component responsible for that heat, but we can certainly feel when it comes into contact with our skin if, for instance, we seed and chop the chiles with bare hands; and it can easily travel to any other ingredient that comes into contact with the cutting board and knife used to cut the chiles, including that apple you were planning to nibble on while you finish cooking dinner. A few simple precautions can help you avoid unexpected and unpleasant encounters with this powerful irritant. In short, wear rubber gloves when handling the chiles and wash the knife and cutting board thoroughly after cutting them. I like to use a dishwasher-safe cutting board for chiles.

THE TAWLES
Building the Table

Everything that led me to now really began at the table, or tawle ("TOW-lah" in Arabic). In the purest sense I mean my childhood table. But in the larger sense I see a "table" in every story I tell. It has become the organizing principle for everything I do.

I feel like we often get recipes for certain dishes but we don't know how to put the whole meal together. And in the case of this cookbook, the dishes really must go together; grilled meats alone would be lost without the sauces—but it really doesn't matter which sauces. I want to share the vision of a meal with no courses, where plates keep coming, getting stacked on top of each other, and everything works together—family style, where everyone breaks bread together.

The style of eating that is common in these regions removes the focus from individual recipes that must be prepared and served according to set rules and turns it instead to building a meal around a few different dishes. The individual recipes in this book are delicious, but the real magic comes when a few or several are served at the same meal, and not necessarily at the same time. Bread is your utensil and the heart of the meal, and the sauces allow diners to make each bite something new. I grew up eating in this mix-and-match way. Dad used to tease Mom about how a table set for dinner couldn't be set without utensils. Mom would shrug as if to ask why our two hands and a bit of bread weren't enough.

Placed at four different spots throughout the book are beautiful visual stories. These tawles are set for celebratory meals, spread with an array of foods and dishes from the book. I think of these tawles a bit like a mannequin in a department store that is appointed with such a perfect outfit you ask the salesperson to pull all the pieces for you and just buy it outright.

1

The Road to Your Favorite Bite

Dipping Sauces

When I was growing up, we didn't use store-bought condiments. Instead, we had most of the sauces in this chapter in our refrigerator! They didn't seem like anything special at the time. Thankfully now I know better. The way we ate then is the way I eat now, the way we serve at Maydān, and the way I hope you'll eat the food in this book. The table is set with several shared platters of foods, small dishes of flavorful sauces, and a big basket of flatbread. Diners tear off a small piece of bread and use it to hold or dip into as many different bits of food and sauces as they'd like. I love to eat this way, because each bite—Mom calls it a *bakoun*—is made up of whatever flavors you choose for yourself. And when there are two or more dipping sauces available, every single bite can offer you a new taste and texture experience. I put this chapter of recipes first because I am convinced that these sauces make every other savory dish in this book taste phenomenal. Hell, they'll make every other savory thing in your kitchen taste phenomenal, period. They're not just sauces; they're a way of life. Often I recommend serving specific sauces with certain dishes, but any combination that sounds good to you will be delicious. And if two or more sauces are available, all the better.

Left: Mountaintop in Lebanon

IN THIS CHAPTER

Top: Exploring the markets of
Muscat, Oman

Right: Lunch with dips in the
mountains, Lebanon

Left: Roadside stop for man'ouche
and sfeeha, Lebanon

Clockwise from top left: Tomato Jam (page 39), Ezme (page 37), Zhough (page 37), Red Shatta (page 38), Harissa (page 35), Tahina (page 34), Chermoula (page 36), Toum (page 34)

Toum

Whipped Garlic Sauce

Makes about 2 cups (480 ml)

½ cup (75 g) peeled, trimmed cloves garlic (about 18 cloves)

1 large egg white, at room temperature (see Note)

2 cups (480 ml) grapeseed or other neutral vegetable oil

¼ cup (60 ml) fresh lemon juice (from about 2 lemons)

¾ teaspoon kosher salt

This sauce is heaven for garlic lovers, and no one else should try it, at least not until it's been in the fridge for a few days so the garlic's bite has mellowed. All that glorious garlic needs a good kick of lemon to balance the flavor. At Maydān, we also add egg whites because we like their fluffy consistency. With a jar of this in your fridge, you need never fear that a dish is too bland for some—just put this on the table and anyone who wants a little zing can add it to their plate.

Using a paring knife, halve the garlic cloves lengthwise and use the tip of the knife to remove the green germ running through the center of each half; discard the germs. Chop the garlic. Transfer the garlic to a food processor and add the egg white.

Pour the oil and lemon juice into a glass measuring cup or other container with a spout for easy pouring.

Pulse the food processor a few times, then with the food processor running, add the oil–lemon juice mixture in a very slow, thin, steady stream until the mixture emulsifies into a cloud. Add the salt and process briefly to combine.

Transfer to a serving container and serve. Refrigerate leftovers in a covered container up to 2 weeks.

Notes: Eggs are easier to separate when they are cold, but egg whites whip best when they are warmer than that. After separating the egg, store the yolk in an airtight container in the refrigerator and use it in a different recipe. Let the egg white stand on the counter until it is at cool room temperature (or at least no longer fresh-from-the-fridge cold).

For a vegan toum, use 2 tablespoons aquafaba (the liquid from cooked or canned chickpeas) in place of the egg white. Note that it will take several minutes for the emulsification to come together.

Tahina

Levantine Tahini–Lemon Sauce

Makes about 1⅓ cups (315 ml)

½ cup (120 ml) tahini (sesame seed paste), preferably Beirut brand, stirred until smooth before measuring

2 tablespoons grapeseed or other neutral vegetable oil

2 tablespoons fresh lemon juice (from about 1 lemon)

1 clove garlic, crushed with garlic press

½ teaspoon kosher salt

This simple sauce is common to the entire region, and it can pretty much go with anything. For lactose-intolerant people, like me, its dairy-free creaminess is very welcome

Place the tahini, oil, lemon juice, garlic, salt, and ½ cup (120 ml) water in a food processor. Process until smooth.

Serve at room temperature or cold. Refrigerate leftovers in a covered container for up to 1 week.

Harissa
North African Red Pepper Sauce

Makes about 2½ cups (600 ml)

1½ pounds (680 g) red bell peppers, halved, seeds and ribs removed, and roasted until very dark (see below)

4 ounces (115 g) serrano peppers, halved, seeds and ribs removed, and roasted until very dark (see below)

½ cup (120 ml) extra-virgin olive oil, preferably Lebanese unfiltered, plus more as needed for serving and storing

¼ cup (60 ml) grapeseed oil

¼ cup (60 ml) fresh lemon juice (from about 2 lemons)

2 tablespoons finely chopped garlic

2 tablespoons Spanish sweet paprika

2 tablespoons Aleppo pepper flakes

2 tablespoons cumin seed, toasted (page 39) and ground

2 teaspoons kosher salt

Harissa is everywhere in Morocco and Tunisia, where this chile pepper paste is used to flavor food before, during, and after it is cooked. When I was there I adopted the local position that no meal is complete without it. Harissa can be very mild, ear-poppingly hot, and everything in between. It looks like a long list of ingredients, but harissa is worth every step. It'll keep for ages, and you'll still be thanking yourself weeks from now if you put the time in today.

Place the peppers in a blender. Add ¼ cup (60 ml) water along with the olive oil, grapeseed oil, lemon juice, garlic, paprika, Aleppo, cumin, and salt. Blend until smooth.

Before using or serving the harissa, you can add more olive oil if you prefer a looser consistency.

To store, transfer to a container with a tight-fitting lid. Smooth the top and pour over enough vegetable or olive oil to cover the surface. Cover the container and refrigerate up to 1 month.

Roasting Peppers and Chiles

Roasting peppers and chiles deepens their flavor and color. As noted on page 25, wear disposable rubber gloves when handling any chiles that have capsaicin and are spicy hot, such as serranos or habaneros, and wash the knife and cutting board thoroughly after cutting them.

***

Fresh bell peppers or other peppers or chiles, halved, seeds and ribs removed

Extra-virgin olive oil, preferably Lebanese unfiltered

***

Preheat the oven to 450°F (230°C).

Place the peppers in a large bowl and drizzle with some olive oil. Toss with your hands until the peppers are well coated all over with oil.

Arrange the peppers cut side down on a baking sheet and roast until browned in spots, 7 to 12 minutes for small, thin chiles or 25 to 30 minutes for large bell peppers.

When a recipe calls for the peppers to be very roasted (as for harissa, above), roast them until they are shriveled and very brown, about 40 minutes for bell peppers; basically, you want to roast them until you look at them and think you've overdone it.

If the recipe calls for the peppers to be peeled after roasting, place them in a bowl and drape a kitchen towel over the top for a few minutes. Use a paring knife to help remove and discard the skin; it should peel off easily. Do not rinse the peppers.

Refrigerate roasted peppers in a tightly covered container for up to 1 day; to refrigerate up to 4 days, pour over enough olive oil to cover the roasted peppers or chiles.

Chermoula

North African Saffron and Herb Sauce

Makes about 3 cups (720 ml)

¼ teaspoon crushed saffron threads

10 cloves garlic, finely chopped

2 bunches fresh flat-leaf parsley, leaves and tender stems, chopped

½ bunch fresh cilantro, leaves and tender stems, chopped

Grated zest of 2 large lemons

5 teaspoons coriander seed, coarsely ground

1 tablespoon Spanish smoked paprika (see Note)

2½ teaspoons red pepper flakes

1 teaspoon ground turmeric

2 teaspoons kosher salt, or to taste

1½ cups (360 ml) grapeseed, canola, or other neutral vegetable oil, plus more as needed for storing

Extra-virgin olive oil, preferably Lebanese unfiltered (optional; for storing)

Chermoula is a common sauce across North Africa, where it's often eaten as an accompaniment to fish. Familiar though it may be in Moroccan, Tunisian, Algerian, and Libyan cooking, how it's made and what ingredients it contains varies widely from town to town, family to family. During our research trip for Maydān, we had excellent chermoula with many of our meals in Tunisia's capital city, Tunis, and the area surrounding the capital. Yet our local friend Aymen was determined that we must taste his aunt's chermoula, which he considers the best in the region. And so we spent a full day driving to and from Sfax, a coastal city located three-and-a-half-hours from Tunis, in order to sample Aymen's aunt's chermoula. Made from caramelized onions and the extracted juice of raisins ground by hand, hers was rich and subtly sweet, and honestly nothing at all like this one. I loved every moment of our excursion that day, but I did not in the end prefer Aymen's aunt's chermoula to the brighter, uncooked types we had in other parts of the country, and which this chermoula is based on. It is herbal and smoky and can go with any and all dishes in this book. For the kind of rich sweetness that the Sfax chermoula made by Aymen's aunt offers, make the Sweet Tomato Jam (page 39)—no hand-grinding required!

Place the saffron threads in 1 tablespoon room temperature water until the threads start to dissolve, about 60 seconds.

In a medium bowl, stir together the garlic, parsley, cilantro, lemon zest, coriander, paprika, red pepper flakes, turmeric, salt, and the saffron in its soaking water.

Transfer the mixture to a food processor; don't overfill the container—do this in batches if necessary. Process while slowly drizzling in the oil until the mixture is well combined and smooth with a little bit of texture, like the consistency of pesto. If doing batches, transfer the first batch to a bowl; process the rest of the mixture with the rest of the oil, then stir the second batch into the first.

To store, transfer to a container with a tight-fitting lid. Smooth the top and pour over enough vegetable or olive oil to cover the surface. Cover the container and refrigerate up to 1 month.

Note: I love the depth and, yes, smokiness that the smoked paprika brings, but if you're nervous about your sauce tasting too strongly of smoke, just add half of it to start, then taste the finished chermoula. You can always stir in more at the end.

Ezme
Turkish "Pico de Gallo"

Makes about 3 cups (720 ml)

6 ripe plum tomatoes (about 1¼ pounds / 570 g), peeled (see page 105) and chopped

½ pint shishito peppers (about 2½ ounces / 70 g), stemmed and chopped

½ large red onion, chopped

½ cup (120 ml) sherry vinegar, plus more as needed

2 tablespoons pomegranate molasses

2 tablespoons ground sumac

1½ teaspoons Aleppo pepper flakes

1 teaspoon kosher salt, plus more as needed

A fresh, chopped tomato salad has been served alongside every kebab I've ever eaten in Turkey, and though it seems ubiquitous, ezme can vary quite a bit in appearance and flavor from place to place, ranging from very chunky to smooth and super bright and from fresh to mellow and macerated. In this way it brings to mind the many kinds of pico de gallo that are served on Mexican dining tables. Maydān's ezme includes some sherry vinegar along with pomegranate molasses to lend a small dose of sweet that tempers the sharp; it's great with grilled or roasted meat or fish.

Place the tomatoes, shishito peppers, and onion in a food processor and pulse a few times until all are finely chopped. Transfer the vegetables to a medium bowl.

In a small bowl, whisk together the vinegar, molasses, sumac, Aleppo pepper flakes, and salt. Pour the dressing over the vegetables and stir gently to combine. Taste and adjust the seasoning with more vinegar or salt.

Serve at room temperature. Refrigerate leftovers in a covered container for up to 2 weeks; let come to room temperature before serving.

Zhough
Chile–Cilantro Sauce

Makes about 3 cups (720 ml)

6 serrano peppers, seeds, ribs, and stems removed, chopped

1 bunch fresh cilantro, leaves and tender stems, chopped

1 bunch fresh flat-leaf parsley, leaves and tender stems, chopped

5 cloves garlic, chopped

1 cup (240 ml) extra-virgin olive oil, preferably Lebanese unfiltered, plus more for storage

¾ cup (180 ml) grapeseed or other neutral vegetable oil, plus more for storage

1 tablespoon cumin seed, ground

1½ teaspoons kosher salt, or to taste

Some of the very best food I've had was in western Oman, on the border with Yemen, where immigrants and refugees from Yemen were cooking traditional Yemeni dishes. At the top of that list of delectable bites is this bright green, garlicky sauce with just a bit of heat. I love it with grilled steak and lamb, and it's an integral part of Maydān's beloved grilled cauliflower dish (page 97).

Place the serranos, cilantro, parsley, garlic, olive oil, vegetable oil, cumin, and salt in a food processor. Process until smooth.

Serve at room temperature. To store, transfer to a container with a tight-fitting lid. Smooth the top and pour over enough olive or vegetable oil to cover the surface. Cover the container and refrigerate up to 1 month.

Red Shatta

Hot Pepper Sauce

Makes about 2 cups (480 ml)

1¼ pounds (570 g) red Fresno chiles (see Note)

1 rounded tablespoon kosher salt (see Note)

1¾ tablespoons apple cider vinegar

2¼ teaspoons sugar

I mostly associate this spicy pepper sauce with Palestine though it is popular throughout the region. Shatta can be made with red chiles, green chiles, or whatever mix you'd like. The amount of heat in the sauce primarily depends on the types of chiles you use. We like to use red Fresno chiles because once they turn red, they have both nice, balanced heat as well as a lovely sweetness. And they're delicious when roasted. If you want a little more heat, you can swap out a small amount of the Fresnos for habanero, but don't overdo it! Finally, shatta can be chunky like a salsa or smooth, like this one. Go ahead and experiment with all of these variables.

In a medium bowl, combine the roasted and unroasted Fresnos and the salt, and then toss and stir to make sure the chiles are thoroughly coated in salt. Transfer to an airtight nonreactive container or zip-top plastic bag and refrigerate for at least 2 days and up to 5 days; once a day, stir the chiles or massage them (if in a bag).

Transfer the chiles and their liquid to a blender. Add the apple cider vinegar and sugar and process until smooth.

Refrigerate in a covered container up to 2 weeks.

Notes: Halve and roast half of the chiles as instructed on page 35 (you can leave some or all of their seeds; there is no need to peel them); and simply halve and remove the seeds from the other half of the chiles, but don't roast them.

I've adapted this recipe from the version that we make at Maydān, which relies on weighing all the ingredients. This volume-based version works very well for a small batch like this one, but if you want to make a larger batch or experiment with different kinds of chiles, use the following weight-based formula for best results: Weigh the trimmed, seeded, and raw (not yet roasted) chiles in grams, then multiply that number by 0.03 (3 percent) to find the amount of salt (for instance, if the weight of the chiles at this stage is 500 grams, you'll add 15 grams salt to them, because 500 x 0.03 = 15). When you're ready to add the vinegar and sugar a few days later, weigh the chiles and all their liquid in grams, then multiply that number by 0.05 (5 percent) to find the amount (weight in grams) of vinegar, and 0.02 (2 percent) to find the amount (weight in grams) of sugar.

Sweet Tomato Jam

Makes about 2 cups (480 ml)

1 can (28 ounces / 795 g) whole plum tomatoes

3 tablespoons (45 ml) extra-virgin olive oil, preferably Lebanese unfiltered

½ medium onion, finely chopped

4 cloves garlic, finely chopped

1 tablespoon tomato paste

3 tablespoons (37.5 g) sugar

3 tablespoons (30 g) white sesame seeds, toasted (see below)

2 (3-inch / 7.5-cm) cinnamon sticks

2 tablespoons distilled white vinegar, or to taste

½ teaspoon kosher salt, or to taste

This is one of the most popular things at Maydān, and it's also one of the very few sweet items that isn't a dessert. This tomato jam is such a customer favorite, in fact, that we put it in jars for our takeout guests during the first Covid Christmas. Maybe it was the comforting aroma of the cinnamon, or that it was a connection to what we call the "before times," or that it is extremely tasty with roasted meats, which people seemed to be eating a lot of in late 2020, but no matter the reason, it made everyone very happy. And it certainly doesn't require a global pandemic to enjoy this at home now, especially considering how easy it is to make. The jam goes especially well with the Ras el Hanout–Rubbed Duck Breast (page 209).

Pour the tomatoes and their juice into a large bowl and finely crush the tomatoes with your hands; alternatively, process the tomatoes in a food processor to chop them. Set aside.

In a large heavy-bottomed pot, heat the olive oil over medium heat. Add the onion and cook, stirring frequently, until softened and translucent, about 8 minutes. Stir in the garlic and cook until softened, about 1 minute. Add the tomato paste and cook, stirring, until darkened in color, about 2 minutes.

Stir in the reserved tomatoes, then the sugar, sesame seeds, and cinnamon sticks. Bring the mixture to a gentle simmer and cook until the flavors have melded, 35 to 45 minutes, stirring frequently to prevent sticking. Reduce the heat as necessary to keep the mixture at a gentle simmer.

Remove the pan from the heat and stir in the vinegar and salt; taste and adjust the seasoning.

Let cool completely. Refrigerate the jam in a tightly covered container up to 2 weeks.

Toasting Seeds and Spices

In a cast-iron or other heavy skillet over medium-low heat, toast seeds or whole spices until they smell fragrant and are lightly browned. Seeds will take 2 to 3 minutes and should be stirred constantly; spices will take 30 to 60 seconds and should be stirred frequently. Immediately transfer toasted seeds or spices to a plate to cool.

2

What We Eat Before We Eat

Mezze, Dips, and Spreads

I always laugh at how the spread my family puts out before dinner easily includes enough food to be a full meal for most people. For us, though, the many bowls and platters full of dips and spreads and olives and pickles and bread are merely the warm-up to the major eating, which only happens once we are all seated at the dinner table (Mom will never embrace buffet-style meals). When the mezze is out, that's when we mingle and catch up with everyone, before we're all in our designated spots for dinner.

My own style of entertaining is a little less structured, and I consider the dips, spreads, and pickles in this chapter fair game for any part of the meal. The recipes are versatile and filling enough to have whatever way works best for you, whether you're eating your meal, or eating before your meal. What's especially wonderful about them is that most can be made ahead of time— in some cases, quite far in advance—which means I get to spend less time in the kitchen and more time with my company. But none of this is possible unless you also provide something to eat it with. Be sure to put out lots of that something, whether it's sliced or torn flatbread (which we always called Syrian bread in my house), baguette, pita chips, crackers, fresh lettuce leaves, sliced cucumbers, or carrot sticks. It can be anything edible, and it absolutely does not need to be homemade!

Left: Lunch from a roadside stand in Oman

IN THIS CHAPTER

Top left: Lunch on the Mediterranean, Bartroun, Lebanon

Bottom left: The ruins in Baalbek, Lebanon

Above: Markets of Muscat, Oman

Sabzi Khordan

Herb Plate

Serves 4

For the cream (optional):

1 jar (6 ounces / 170 g) clotted cream or labne (see Note)

2 to 3 tablespoons whey from a jar of shanklish or other fresh cheese, such as mozzarella (optional)

1 teaspoon freshly grated orange zest

1 tablespoon honey

Kosher salt

1 bunch green onions

¼ to ½ bunch fresh flat-leaf parsley, gently rinsed and dried

¼ to ½ bunch fresh mint, gently rinsed and dried

¼ to ½ bunch fresh dill, gently rinsed and dried

The name *sabzi khordan* comes from Iran, but I first had it in Georgia, where they serve the platter of fresh cheese and herbs with delightful little pickled sprouts and/or flowers called jonjoli. A plate of herbs, fresh onion, fresh or pickled vegetables, and sometimes a thick cream or soft cheese is served in many parts of the Caucasus as well as Turkey and Lebanon, though what exactly is on the plate changes depending on what's in season. In my experience, across much of the region the plate of herbs is left on the table throughout the meal. Diners can customize each bite by picking off or scooping up any combination of herb, onion, and, if included, cream or cheese they'd like to add to whatever else is in their bread; these little extras heighten the flavor of everything that is being eaten. And, honestly, it's just refreshing to nibble on a bit of fresh herb as a palate cleanser at any time. I admit to some frustration at Maydān, where we have yet to convince a majority of diners to embrace using the things on this plate to add freshness and flavor to any bite throughout the meal. Too often it just sits there, which is a real shame. We're hopeful that if we just keep trying, we might eventually create a little revolution of taste for our diners and win over their hearts and minds.

Here I suggest the fresh ingredients that are generally easiest to find year-round in the United States, but by all means use whatever is freshest and in season, and that has a flavor you love. Interesting choices beyond what's listed at left include chervil, chives, tarragon, fennel fronds, lovage, shiso, Chinese celery, and cilantro flowers. You can make it as elaborate (or simple) as you like, and feel free to omit the flavored cream.

To make the cream, if using, in a medium bowl gently whisk together the cream, whey, orange zest, honey, and salt to taste. (You'll have about ¾ cup / 180 ml.) Cover and store in the refrigerator until ready to use, or up to 4 days.

To prepare the green onions, trim their tops and ends and peel off and discard any tough outer layer.

When ready to serve, if using the cream, scrape it into a small serving bowl and place it on a serving platter. Arrange the green onions and herbs on the platter.

Pass the platter around the table and encourage diners to take a little of everything so that they can add bits of the cream, green onion, and herbs to their bites of food in any combination they like.

Note: I've seen lots of different types of fresh cheese used in sabzi khordan; clotted cream has a little less tang than labne, and either works well here.

Beet Borani

Makes about 3½ cups (840 ml);
serves 4 to 6

1½ pounds (680 g) red beets

Extra-virgin olive oil, preferably Lebanese
unfiltered

1 clove garlic, minced

1 cup (250 ml) labne or, if unavailable, full-fat
Greek yogurt

1½ teaspoons fresh lemon juice (optional if
using the Greek yogurt)

Kosher salt

Fresh dill, for garnish

Black or white sesame seeds, for garnish

Bread or crudités, for serving

I grew up happily eating and truly loving beets. Then came our time in Russia. During those three years I had so many bowls of borscht that this beet lover turned into a beet loather. I knew it would require a miracle for me to ever again consider eating beets after that. Happily, miracles can happen, and this one came in the form of a stunning Iranian yogurt-and-beet dip, which tastes as good as it looks. This Iranian yogurt dip is a lot like the m'tabbals from the Levant (page 48). I believe the main difference between them is that borani is made with yogurt and m'tabbal with tahini, but I'm sorry I've not yet been able to travel to Iran to see for myself. Thankfully we have a few very dear Iranian friends in Washington and Los Angeles, and over the years they have helped us understand a little about how many of these cross-lingual dishes are served in their home country. You can make either boranis or m'tabbals with all sorts of different vegetables, which makes both of them excellent ways to use up veggies that might otherwise languish in your crisper drawer or get tossed out. I'm especially fond of those made with spinach or eggplant, but none can match the striking pink color of this one.

Preheat the oven to 425°F (220°C). Trim and scrub the beets. Place them in a large cast-iron skillet and drizzle with olive oil just to coat. Cover the skillet with aluminum foil and seal it around the ends of the pan. Roast until very tender when pierced with a thin, sharp knife, about 1½ hours. Remove from the oven and let stand until cool enough to handle.

Peel, then coarsely chop the cooled beets. Place half of the chopped beets in a blender with about half of the minced garlic. Purée until mostly smooth. Add ¼ cup (60 ml) labne and purée until smooth. Transfer to a medium bowl.

Repeat the process to purée the remaining beets and garlic. Whisk in any remaining labne or yogurt by hand. Whisk in the lemon juice, if using. Season with salt to taste. Garnish with the dill and sesame seeds. Serve with bread or crudités.

Store the borani in a tightly covered container in the refrigerator up to 2 weeks.

M'tabbal
Dulu' el-Selek
Swiss Chard Dip

Makes about 3 cups (720 ml);
serves 4 to 6

2 large bunches Swiss chard

2 tablespoons neutral oil, such as canola or grapeseed

5 cloves garlic, sliced

Kosher salt

Juice of 1 lemon (about 3 tablespoons)

½ cup (120 ml) pourable tahini (sesame seed paste), preferably Beirut brand, stirred until smooth before measuring

Toné (page 123) or other flat bread, for serving

Crudités, for serving

M'tabbal, which means "tossed" or "stirred" in Arabic, is a popular style of dip often made with eggplant and tahini. If that sounds to you like another familiar dip from the region, note that I've been told that baba ghanoush (Mom's is on page 56) is an eggplant salad while m'tabbal is an eggplant sesame dip. We don't have to worry too much about that distinction because this version of m'tabbal is made with Swiss chard. Honestly it began at Maydān as a clever way to use up a bunch of Swiss chard stems left over after the leaves were used in another dish; we hate to waste anything edible if we can help it. Then it turned into one of our guests' favorite dips (and not only because it's lactose-free—also because it's delicious)! For those of us who cook in a home kitchen, it's generally easiest (and tastiest) to use both leaves and stems, but don't hesitate to use just those stems if the leaves have found their way into a different pot.

Remove the stems from the Swiss chard leaves. Thinly slice the stems and tear the leaves; set both aside separately.

In a large sauté pan, heat the oil over medium heat. Add the reserved sliced Swiss chard stems and the garlic along with a couple pinches of salt. Cook, stirring frequently, until softened, about 5 minutes; control the heat so the garlic does not brown (you want it to be soft, not crispy).

Add the leaves and cook, frequently tossing them with tongs, until the leaves are completely wilted and both leaves and stems are very tender. Remove the pan from the heat and set aside until completely cool.

Transfer the cooled Swiss chard to a food processor. Pulse a few times to finely chop the mixture. Add the lemon juice, ¼ cup (60 ml) water, and a pinch of salt and process until puréed. With the food processor running, stream in the tahini and process until smooth and blended.

Transfer to a bowl and cover and chill before serving or up to 3 days. Let stand at room temperature a few minutes before serving with bread and crudités.

Labne
with Dried Mint

Makes about 2 cups (475 ml);
serves 4 to 6

1 container (16 ounces / 455 g) labne

2½ tablespoons dried mint

1 teaspoon fresh lemon juice, or as needed

1 tablespoon extra-virgin olive oil, preferably
Lebanese unfiltered

Kosher salt

As ubiquitous as labne was in our Lebanese-American kitchen,
I can't recall ever being persuaded to take even one bite of it.
Other than mozzarella, which I ate by the fistful, I was firmly a
"no dairy" kid. I simply didn't like it. Today, I like to eat all kinds
of dairy (lactose intolerance notwithstanding; see page 229), but
labne is the one I love the most. In this mixture, the flavor of the
dried mint and the texture from the whisking combine to make
it the most light and refreshing labne dip I've had. If I had to
choose one thing and one thing only to eat with the roasted lamb
shoulder (page 200), it would be this labne, every time. Thankfully
I've never been put in this position. One key to keeping the
texture light is to whisk gently; if you whisk too vigorously or too
long, the sauce may turn soupy.

In a medium bowl, gently whisk together the labne, mint, and lemon juice.
Whisking constantly at a moderate speed (remember, don't whisk too
vigorously or the sauce may turn soupy), slowly stream in the oil.

Taste and add salt or more lemon juice as desired.

Cover and chill if not using at once and up to 4 days. Let stand at room
temperature for a few minutes before serving.

Clockwise from top left: Labne
with Dried Mint (this page),
Taktouka (page 58), M'tabbal Dulu'
el-Selek (opposite)

Hummus, Three Ways

Makes about 6 cups (1.4 liters);
serves 10 to 14

1 cup (250 ml) fresh lemon juice (from about
6 lemons)

½ cup (120 ml) extra-virgin olive oil, preferably
Lebanese unfiltered, plus more for serving

6 cloves garlic

4 cups (740 g) cooked, drained chickpeas
(see page 52)

1 cup (240 ml) pourable tahini (sesame seed
paste), preferably Beirut brand, stirred until
smooth before measuring

1½ teaspoons kosher salt, or to taste

¼ cup (60 ml) reserved cooking liquid from
chickpeas, or as needed

Ground sumac, for garnish

Before I was tall enough to reach the countertops I had two important jobs in the kitchen: running drained chickpeas through the Foley food mill and scraping out the tahini jar. I'm not sure what qualified me for the first job (and today I use a food processor, as it is way easier), but for the second one I'm pretty sure it was being the only person with arms that were long and skinny enough, and a spirit that was obsessive enough, to get every last drop of tahini from the bottom of the jar.

Perhaps it was all that time I spent with my arm in a tahini jar that made me particularly sensitive to this particular ingredient, but I feel strongly that thick, over-tahini'd hummus is terrible. I know there's an argument to be made (and plenty make it) that using dried chickpeas is the defining difference between good and great hummus, but I've learned that even that important choice isn't nearly as impactful as the tahini. My favorite brand is Beirut, and it helps to make this hummus one of the smoothest and creamiest you'll ever have. This hummus is also one of the lightest I've had, thanks in part to blending a bit of the chickpea cooking liquid (called *aquafaba*) into the finished hummus. The recipe here yields hummus that is fantastic served simply, with nothing more than olive oil and sumac on top. Or, if you'd like to jazz it up, two variations follow, one with fresh vegetables and the other with pulled lamb. Hence the name, Hummus, Three Ways!

In a blender, place the lemon juice, olive oil, and garlic and blend to combine. Add the chickpeas and blend until very smooth. Add the tahini (see Note) and process until well combined.

Season with salt and process to combine. Add up to ¼ cup (60 ml) of the reserved chickpea cooking liquid and process; this creates some nice air bubbles and lightens the texture of the hummus.

To serve, transfer to a serving bowl. Use the back of a spoon to make a shallow divot in the surface of the hummus. Pour some olive oil into the divot and sprinkle with sumac.

Store in a covered container in the refrigerator up to 5 days.

Note: If you're using a chunky or very stiff tahini, it'll probably work better to transfer the chickpea mixture out of the blender and into a food processor before adding the tahini. If using Beirut brand or another nice, smooth, pourable tahini, doing it all in the blender is fine.

Beiruti Hummus

Makes about 4½ cups (1 liter);
serves 6 to 8

3 cups (720 ml) Hummus (page 51)

1 cup (240 ml) quartered cherry tomatoes

½ cup (75 g) very thinly sliced shishito peppers
(no need to seed them)

½ cup (50 g) very thinly sliced green onion,
greens only (from 2 to 3 bunches)

Extra-virgin olive oil, preferably Lebanese
unfiltered, for serving

The moment in Beirut when my Maydān team and I tasted this dish for the first time, we all knew at once that we would be bringing it to the restaurant. The tomatoes, peppers, and green onions mixed in with the creamy hummus were so fresh and crisp. The only caveat is that this isn't nearly as good when made with out-of-season regular tomatoes, which are far too watery and make the whole thing a runny mess. That's why I call for cherry tomatoes here—to try to mitigate against this unpleasant result no matter what time of year it is. If it's the height of summer, however, you can (and should!) chop up the brightest, ripest tomatoes you can find for this refreshing dip.

Place the hummus in a large bowl. Just before serving, fold in the tomatoes, shishitos, and green onions.

Transfer to a serving bowl. Drizzle over some olive oil just before serving.

Once combined, this is best eaten the day it is made; the tomatoes in particular may give up some liquid if stored.

Chickpeas

Makes about 6 cups (1 kg) drained chickpeas

Because chickpeas are used in so many different ways throughout the region (and this book), I typically don't salt them during initial cooking so that I have more control over the seasoning when using them in a dish. Adding baking soda during cooking helps the beans to cook more quickly. If you are preparing the chickpeas for a particular recipe and you know this amount of dry will give you less or more than you need, you can certainly double or halve the recipe as needed. Alternatively, you may use the extras in another dish or put the chickpeas and enough of their cooking liquid to cover them in a tightly closed container and freeze for up to 3 months.

***

1 pound (455 g) dried chickpeas

¾ teaspoon baking soda

***

Rinse and drain chickpeas and place in a large pot. Add 1½ quarts (1.4 liters) of water and soak for 24 hours. (It's fine to skip this step; the chickpeas will simply take longer to cook—perhaps twice as long.)

Drain the chickpeas and return them to the pot. Add 3 quarts (2.8 liters) of water and the baking soda. Bring to a boil over high heat. Partially cover the pot and boil gently until the chickpeas are fork tender, 30 to 45 minutes, depending on the age of the chickpeas and how you are using them. For the hummus, cook them until they are almost falling apart. For Dango (page 153) or a similar dish where they'll be cooked further, cook the chickpeas until just tender. For salads and other stand-alone purposes, cook until they are tender but still keep their shape.

Let them cool in the cooking liquid. Store in the liquid in a tightly covered container in the refrigerator up to 4 days; freeze up to 3 months. When draining the chickpeas before using them in a dish, make sure to save some cooking liquid if it's called for in the recipe.

Hummus bil Lahme
Hummus with Meat

Serves 8 to 12

4 cups (about 2 pounds / 940 g) pulled meat from Maydān's Lamb Shoulder with Syrian Seven Spice (page 200; see Note)

¼ cup (½ stick / 115 g) unsalted butter

½ cup (120 ml) Harissa (page 35)

1 cup (240 ml) fresh orange juice (from about 3 oranges)

1 tablespoon fresh lemon juice

1 tablespoon kosher salt

4 cups (960 ml) Hummus (page 51)

Putting meat on top of hummus is such a great trick for quickly making a nourishing and very tasty meal. I like spooning hashwee (the filling for the Kibbeh Sanieh, page 199) on top of hummus, and I've been known to quickly cook some onion and cubed lamb in butter to eat the same way.

Now if you have a little bit of time, here's another way to turn hummus into a full meal, and this one is good enough to serve to company. Simmering pulled lamb in a mixture that includes harissa and fresh orange juice makes the lamb melt-in-your-mouth delicious; it's a delectable way to use up any leftover pulled meat or poultry. I don't think I'm giving away state secrets by sharing that this combination of pulled lamb and hummus is former president Obama's favorite item on the Maydān menu. When he lived full-time in DC, we always made sure to have it when he came in. In fairness, this was far easier to do for him than for anyone else, since we always had plenty of warning before he ate with us!

Place the pulled lamb in a large saucepan. Add the butter, harissa, orange juice, lemon juice, and salt. Heat over low heat for 30 minutes.

To serve, place the hummus in a large shallow bowl and top with the lamb. To plate this as individual servings, put about ⅔ cup (165 ml) hummus in a small shallow dish or ramekin and top with about ½ cup (4 ounces / 115 g) pulled lamb.

Note: To pull the lamb, place the cooked shoulder in a large bowl and use two forks to pull it apart; this is easier to do if the lamb is slightly warmed first.

Muhammara

Walnut, Roasted Red Pepper, and Pomegranate Dip

Makes 4 cups (960 ml); serves 6 to 8

13 ounces (370 g) walnuts (about 3¾ cups), toasted (see below)

2½ pounds (1.2 kg) red bell peppers (about 6), cored, seeded, roasted (see page 354), and chopped (see Note)

1 can (6 ounces / 170 g) tomato paste

⅔ cup (165 ml) extra-virgin olive oil, preferably Lebanese unfiltered, plus more for serving

⅓ cup (75 ml) pomegranate molasses, plus more for serving

1½ to 2 tablespoons fresh lemon juice

2½ tablespoons sweet paprika

5 cloves garlic, minced

Kosher salt

Chopped fresh chives, for serving

This is a staple on the Lebanese table, but it's not one that I grew up with. This is funny to me because my family loves and uses every ingredient in this dip. It might just be that no one in my great-grandparents' villages made anything like this, and so no recipe was handed down. For me, the best part of this might be the sour note that the pomegranate molasses gives. If you buy muhammara in a store, it's typically quite chunky, but this one, from Maydān's menu, is much thinner and smoother, and I like it best that way.

In a large bowl, toss the toasted walnuts and roasted peppers together.

In a medium bowl, whisk together the tomato paste, olive oil, pomegranate molasses, 1½ tablespoons lemon juice, paprika, garlic, and a few pinches of salt. Pour this liquid mixture over the walnuts and peppers and toss to coat.

In a food processor, process the walnut-and-pepper mixture in batches until the muhammara is blended but still a little chunky. Transfer each batch to a bowl and stir the batches together as you go. Taste and adjust the lemon juice and salt to taste.

Transfer to a serving bowl. With the back of a spoon, press a divot into the top of the dip. Pour a little olive oil and pomegranate molasses in the divot. Garnish with chives and serve.

Store the muhammara in a tightly covered container in the refrigerator up to 1 week.

Note: There is no need to peel the peppers for this blended dip.

Toasting Nuts

Preheat the oven to 350°F (175°C).

Spread nuts on a rimmed baking sheet. Toast in the oven until the nuts smell fragrant and are slightly browned, 5 to 7 minutes, stirring once or twice. Nuts won't always look browner on the outside even when they're toasting on the inside, so I generally depend on my nose before my eyes. If you're not sure, carefully taste a nut. If it tastes toasted, take them out.

Transfer the nuts to a plate to cool.

Mom's Baba Ghanoush

Lebanese Eggplant Dip

Makes about 3 cups (720 ml);
serves 4 to 6

2 medium eggplant (3 to 4 pounds /
1.4 to 1.8 kg)

3 to 4 tablespoons (45 to 60 ml) tahini
(sesame seed paste), preferably Beirut brand,
stirred until smooth before measuring

2 cloves garlic, crushed with garlic press

1 teaspoon kosher salt, plus more as needed

Juice of 1½ to 2 lemons

Ground sumac or chopped fresh parsley,
for garnish (optional)

Most recipes for baba ghanoush will look more or less like the one here, but the most important quality in an excellent version isn't in the ingredient list at all: smoke. If I can't taste the smoke, I think something is wrong. You need a live fire any way you can get it—grill, fireplace, camping stove, even the flame on your gas-powered stovetop! One or more whole eggplant sizzling directly on top of the burner was a regular sight in my house when I was growing up, and in time I came to understand and appreciate why. It's the difference between good and great baba ghanoush.

Use a paring knife to cut several small slits all over the eggplant; this releases the air and helps the eggplant cook evenly.

Remove the grate from the largest gas burner on the stovetop and turn it on to high heat. Place the eggplant directly on the flame, either alongside it or right on top of the burner cap; you can do both eggplant at the same time if you have the space and the inclination. Use long-handled tongs to turn the eggplant as needed and cook until the skin is charred all over and they are very tender when poked with a sharp knife, about 30 minutes.

Alternatively, cook the eggplant over a medium-high grill, turning occasionally, until cooked as described above.

Set the eggplant aside on a baking sheet or plate until cool.

Slice the eggplant in half lengthwise. Scoop out the cooked pulp and place in a bowl; discard the skin. Mash the pulp with a fork or sturdy silicone or rubber spatula; the consistency should be mashed but still coarse.

Stir in the tahini, garlic, and salt. Add the lemon juice a little at a time, tasting as you add it to ensure the mixture isn't too tart; add more salt if necessary.

Transfer to a serving bowl, sprinkle with sumac or garnish with parsley, and serve. Or cover and refrigerate until needed or up to 1 week. For best flavor, let the baba ghanoush sit out for about 30 minutes before garnishing and serving.

Taktouka

Moroccan Roasted Pepper and Tomato Spread

Makes about 3 cups (720 ml);
serves 4

6 tablespoons (90 ml) extra-virgin olive oil,
preferably Lebanese unfiltered, plus more
for serving

2½ pounds (1.2 kg) green bell peppers (about 6),
cored, seeded, roasted (see page 35), peeled,
and diced

1¼ pounds (570 g) ripe plum tomatoes
(about 5), grated on the large holes of a
box grater

½ large onion, thinly sliced lengthwise

3 cloves garlic, minced

2½ tablespoons sweet paprika

1½ tablespoons cumin seed, toasted
(page 39) and ground

1½ teaspoons kosher salt, plus more as needed

Chopped fresh flat-leaf parsley, for serving

Flatbread or sliced baguette, for serving

Like the fresh tomato-and-pepper salad, Ezme (page 37), and the rich, cooked tomato-and-pepper dish, Shakshuka (page 87), taktouka is a spread that highlights the ripe tomatoes and peppers that are the backbone of so much of the cuisine from this part of the world. Scented and flavored with spoonfuls of sweet paprika and toasted cumin, taktouka (which you can see on page 49) is typically served with generous servings of bread, which you'll want and need to finish up every last bit.

In a medium sauté pan with a lid, place the oil, peppers, tomatoes, onion, garlic, paprika, cumin, and the salt. Bring to a simmer over medium heat.

Cover the pan and cook until the onion is softened and the tomatoes have given up a lot of liquid, about 15 minutes; stir occasionally and adjust the heat as necessary to avoid burning on the bottom of the pan.

Uncover the pan, increase the heat to medium-high, and simmer until the liquid is reduced and the mixture is slightly thickened, about 20 minutes, stirring occasionally to prevent sticking on the bottom of the pan. Taste and add more salt if necessary.

Serve warm or cold. To serve, transfer to a serving bowl or platter and smooth the top. Use the back of a spoon to lightly press a slight divot on the surface of the taktouka and pour in some olive oil. Garnish with parsley and serve with bread on the side.

Bamia

Okra and Tomatoes

Serves 6 to 8

2 pounds (910 g) fresh okra, cut lengthwise in half

3 cups (435 g) cherry tomatoes, quartered

2 medium onions, thinly sliced lengthwise

5 cloves garlic, sliced

1 tablespoon whole coriander, toasted (page 39) and ground

2 teaspoons kosher salt plus more as needed

Extra-virgin olive oil, preferably Lebanese unfiltered

2 bunches fresh cilantro, leaves and tender stems, chopped

Juice of ½ to 1 lemon

Traditionally made with lamb throughout the region, Lebanese bamia is typically a hearty okra-and-tomato stew. At Maydān, we serve this fresh and crisp all-vegetable mezze version. Curiously I never tasted okra until I was an adult. I chalk it up to being a family of Lebanese Midwesterners, emphasis on the last part. Okra just wasn't on our radar. Maybe that's why I like this okra dish so much. When lightly roasted, it's crunchy and flavorful, with delightful little seeds that are fun to pop between your teeth.

Preheat the oven to 375°F (190°C).

In a large bowl, place the okra, tomatoes, onions, garlic, and coriander. Add the salt and drizzle over about ¼ cup (60 ml) olive oil. Toss gently until the vegetables are well coated with oil and the salt and coriander are well dispersed.

Spread the vegetables on two rimmed baking sheets and roast until softened and lightly browned in spots, about 15 minutes.

Transfer the roasted vegetables to a bowl and add the cilantro (keep a little aside for garnish) and the juice of ½ lemon. Toss to combine, and taste and adjust the seasoning with more lemon juice and/or salt.

Serve warm. Refrigerate leftovers in an airtight container up to 4 days.

Marinated Olives, Two Ways

We can buy lots of different kinds of seasoned olives at the store, but sometimes I prefer my own combinations of flavors. Here are two of my favorites. I love to use the Moroccan spice blend called ras el hanout on olives because they marry beautifully with the earthy bitterness from spices like turmeric and mustard and the sweetness of spices like cinnamon, mace, and allspice. And in the second recipe below, olives warmed with anise seed, caraway, and olive oil take on a nutty, licorice-y flavor that storebought mixes don't typically have.

Use any kind of unseasoned cured olives for these, such as a combination of Castelvetrano, salt-cured black, and Zorzalena olives, or start with an already-combined "Tunisian" or "Mediterranean" olive mix. Whichever olives you choose, make sure they're unpitted (that is, they still have the pits); this helps ensure they'll hold their shape better.

Ras el Hanout Olives

Makes about 4 cups (620 grams)

1 to 1¼ pounds (455 to 570 g) well-drained mixed olives with pits

½ cup (120 ml) extra-virgin olive oil, preferably Lebanese unfiltered

½ cup (120 ml) neutral vegetable oil, such as grapeseed oil

½ cup (50 g) ras el hanout

2 cloves garlic, shaved or very thinly sliced

Zest of 1 orange, removed with a vegetable peeler and thinly sliced

Place the olives in a large bowl.

In a large glass measuring cup or another bowl, combine the olive oil, vegetable oil, ras el hanout, garlic, and orange zest. Whisk until well combined.

Pour the oil mixture over the olives and toss until very well and evenly combined. Transfer to a glass or other container and cover tightly. Refrigerate for at least 48 hours and up to 1 month.

Let stand at room temperature for at least 30 minutes before serving.

Roasted Anise and Caraway Olives

Makes about 4 cups (620 grams)

1 to 1¼ pounds (455 to 570 g) well-drained mixed olives with pits

¼ cup (25 g) anise seed

2 tablespoons caraway seed

1 cup (240 ml) extra-virgin olive oil, preferably Lebanese unfiltered

½ cup (120 ml) fresh lemon juice (from about 4 lemons)

Preheat the oven to 400°F (205°C).

Place the olives in a large bowl. Add the anise seed, caraway seed, oil, and lemon juice and toss until well coated. Transfer to a rimmed baking sheet and roast until the olives are hot and wrinkled, about 10 minutes.

Use a slotted spoon to transfer the olives to a serving bowl. Serve warm.

Clockwise from top left: Pickled
Cucumbers (page 62), Lift (page 63),
Ras el Hanout Olives (opposite), Pickled
Green Tomatoes (page 63), Roasted
Anise and Caraway Olives (opposite)

Mouneh

*Pickled Cucumbers, Turnips,
and Green Tomatoes*

Every area in the world where humans have endured, it is thanks in part to our ingenious methods of preserving fresh foods so there is something to eat when natural food sources are scarce or simply dormant for the season. Some of these preservation techniques are more toothsome than others, and pickling is certainly among the tastiest of all, which might be part of why pickles, or mouneh, as they're called in Lebanon, are such an important part of the mezze table. Mouneh was an important part of our family's table, too, but this might be because we grew many more cucumbers than we could eat in salads (see below).

Whether you enjoy the idea of pickling your favorite vegetables in season to enjoy later or you're a year-round enthusiast of pickled anything, these three simple recipes will help you transform your veggies from fresh to puckery goodness in very little time. And if you're already an experienced pickler, I hope you'll find here some new ideas for flavor combinations.

Pickled Cucumbers

Makes 2 (1-quart / 960-ml) jars

2 pounds (910 g) pickling cucumbers, quartered lengthwise

4 sprigs dill

½ cup (120 ml) distilled white vinegar

1½ tablespoons apple cider vinegar

2 cloves garlic, smashed with the side of a chef's knife or with a pan

2 tablespoons kosher salt

2 teaspoons coriander seed

2 teaspoons dill seed

1 teaspoon black peppercorns

2 juniper berries

2 whole cloves

2 bay leaves

Equipment: 2 sterilized 1-quart (960-ml) canning jars, lids, and rings (see page 105)

When I was a kid, we grew just one kind of cucumber and used it for eating and pickling. It's common to advise using "pickling" cucumbers these days, which are shorter and broader than regular cucumbers, and have thinner skins. But the regular cucumbers make great pickles, too.

Divide the quartered cucumbers and sprigs of dill between the two canning jars. Push them in tightly, but do not fill more than ½ inch (12 mm) from the top of the jars.

In a small saucepan combine 2 cups (480 ml) water with the distilled vinegar, apple cider vinegar, garlic, salt, coriander seed, dill seed, peppercorns, juniper berries, cloves, and bay leaves.

Bring to a boil over medium heat. Reduce the heat and simmer for 10 minutes. Cover the pan, remove it from the heat, and let stand for 10 minutes.

Bring the mixture just back to a boil, then strain it into the jars, again making sure that you don't go higher than ½ inch (12 mm) from the top of the jars. Discard the solids.

Tighten the lids on top of the jars and let come to room temperature.

Place the jars in the refrigerator for at least 2 days before eating the pickles. Store in the refrigerator 6 months to a year.

Lift
Pickled Turnips

Makes 2 (1-quart / 960-ml) jars

4 medium turnips (about 1½ pounds / 680 g), scrubbed, trimmed, and cut into small wedges

1 medium beet (about 6 ounces / 170 g), scrubbed and cut into 8 wedges

A few slices white onion (optional)

2 tablespoons kosher salt

1½ cups (360 ml) distilled white vinegar

Equipment: 2 sterilized 1-quart (960-ml) canning jars, lids, and rings (see page 105)

I really didn't want anything to do with turnips when I was a kid. Any other pickle was fine, just not this one. It was always there, and I always avoided it. Then I grew up, thankfully, and I learned how much there is to appreciate about earthy, tangy, crispy pickled turnips. The addition of some white onion comes from my grandfather's side. My mother didn't usually do it, preferring the simpler version from her mother's family. But many people like the extra layer of flavor the onion gives, so it's here in case you'd like to try it.

Place a handful of turnip wedges into each jar, followed by 1 beet wedge and a slice of onion, if using. Repeat these rows until you have used all the ingredients. As you get closer to the top, you can push down on the vegetables to make room for a few more, but don't go higher than ½ inch (12 mm) from the top of the jar.

Add 1 tablespoon salt to each jar.

In a small saucepan combine the vinegar with ¾ cup (180 ml) water. Bring to a gentle boil. Divide the hot liquid between the jars.

Tighten the lids on top and place the jars in the refrigerator for at least 3 to 5 days before eating the pickles. Store in the refrigerator 6 months to a year.

Pickled Green Tomatoes

Makes 2 (1-quart / 960-ml) jars

2 pounds (910 g) unripened (green) tomatoes, each cut into 8 wedges

2 sprigs fresh dill

1 cup (240 ml) distilled white vinegar

4 cloves garlic

4 serrano peppers, halved lengthwise

4 bay leaves

2 tablespoons kosher salt

2 teaspoons sugar

Equipment: 2 sterilized 1-quart (960-ml) canning jars, lids, and rings (see page 105)

In my family, the only thing we did with unripe green tomatoes was wait for them to turn red! Thankfully the lovely chefs at Maydān grew up pickling them, and this is how we do it now.

Divide the tomato wedges and dill sprigs between the canning jars, lightly pressing down if necessary to fit as many as possible into the jar, but do not fill more than ½ inch (12 mm) from the top of the jar.

In a small saucepan, combine 1½ cups (360 ml) water with the distilled vinegar, garlic, peppers, bay leaves, salt, and sugar. Bring to a boil, and stir to be sure the sugar and salt are dissolved. Divide the liquid and all of the aromatics between the jars, again making sure that you don't go higher than ½ inch (12 mm) from the top of the jars.

Tighten the lids on top of the jars and let come to room temperature.

Place the jars in the refrigerator for at least 2 days before eating the pickles. Store in the refrigerator 6 months to a year.

Za'atar Martini

Serves 1; makes about 1 cup (240 ml) sumac oil, enough for almost infinite cocktails (see Note)

For the sumac oil:
½ cup (120 ml) untoasted sesame oil

½ cup (120 ml) avocado oil

2 tablespoons ground sumac

For each cocktail:
Ice, for shaking

2 ounces (60 ml) gin

1 ounce (30 ml) dry vermouth

1 barspoon brine from za'atar olives

3 drops sumac oil

Za'atar olive, for garnish

Equipment: Nick and Nora glass

Here is my spin on the classic martini, spiced up with a bit of Maydān flair by way of a little salt and bitter. Cheers to that!

To make the sumac oil, in a small saucepan, heat the sesame oil and avocado oil over low heat until barely bubbling. Add the sumac and cook for 3 minutes, stirring frequently.

Remove the pan from the heat and let cool completely. Strain the oil through a fine-mesh sieve, then transfer to a dropper bottle. Keep at room temperature for up to 1 month or refrigerate for up to 6 months (let come to room temperature before using).

Fill a large cocktail mixing glass with ice. Pour in the gin, vermouth, and olive brine. Stir several times until the outside of the glass feels too cold to hold.

Place a za'atar olive in a Nick and Nora glass. Strain the drink into the glass. Add 3 drops sumac oil. Serve cold, right away!

Note: Or, if infinite martinis are just too many martinis, you can drizzle the sumar oil over the hummus (page 51) or baba ghanoush (page 56) or use it in place of some of the oil when making muhammara (page 55) or chermoula (page 36).

MEZZE TABLE

When I was growing up, mezze were an integral part of every gathering that involved food—and every gathering involved food. Before any guests arrived, our large dining table would be laid with so many pickles, dips, breads, and finger foods that it was nearly impossible to catch even a glimpse of the pretty needlepointing on the tablecloth under all the plates, bowls, and platters. This abundance certainly stemmed from the sweet sentiment my mother carries with her that no one should ever be in her home without something delicious to eat or sip in their hand. And it underscored for my child self that in my family we take the business of feeding people and eating very seriously—so much so that we serve a full meal before the meal!

Like many people, I carried my favorite traditions from my childhood into my adulthood, and I am proud to say that I have a very strong mezze game. I came into this talent honestly, absorbing from Mom the conviction that a person shouldn't spend one moment in my home without food or drink. But even more than that, a huge mezze spread removes any obstacle to the most fun part of the party, which is settling in and talking to my guests.

And unlike my family, in my home, mezze doesn't always precede a meal; sometimes it is the meal. I admit that this is sometimes because I'm having so much fun that I completely forget to put dinner in the oven. But it's also because running my restaurants keeps me so busy that I find that noshing with my friends is often a far more satisfying way to spend my rare evenings at home, and there's no need to ever break up the fun by asking everyone to move and reassemble in a different part of the house for a meal.

Left: Dips and spreads in Lebanon

TAWLE MENU

Sabzi Khordan (Herb Plate), 44

◆

Beet Borani, 47

◆

M'tabbal Dulu' el-Selek
(Swiss Chard Dip), 48

◆

Labne with Dried Mint, 49

◆

Hummus, Three Ways, 51

◆

Muhammara
(Walnut, Roasted Red Pepper,
and Pomegranate Dip), 55

◆

Mom's Baba Ghanoush
(Lebanese Eggplant Dip), 56

◆

Bamia (Okra and Tomatoes), 59

Marinated Olives, Two Ways, 60

◆

Mouneh (Pickled Turnips, Cucumbers,
Green Tomatoes), 62

◆

The Kelly Girls' Tabbouleh, 75

◆

Toum, 34

◆

Syrian cheese

◆

Basturma (spiced, cured beef)

◆

Pita

◆

Arak (anise-flavored,
grape-based distilled spirit)

Salala, Oman

3

From the Fields

Sulta/Salads, Vegetables, and Dolmas

When my mom was a kid, her dad's older brothers owned and operated a fruit and vegetable stand at Detroit's Eastern Market, which was a bustling center of commerce for the wholesale food industry in the early to mid-twentieth century. I think it makes sense that they ended up in the produce business, considering that their own parents had been farmers in their native Lebanon before emigrating to the United States in the very early 1900s. Mom and her sisters have often talked about how, although money was very tight when they were young, there were always plenty of fruits and vegetables available in their house, thanks to a steady supply of "seconds"—the bruised or blemished items that the uncles couldn't sell. Perhaps this would have turned other children off, but it seems to have instilled in my mom an abiding sense that every main meal must include both a cooked and a fresh vegetable. I guess it may have happened, but I can't recall a single night when we didn't have both as part of our dinner. Mom's cooked vegetables and fresh salads were deliciously simple, just like the recipes in this chapter.

IN THIS CHAPTER

Top left: Drinking wine in the mountains, Lebanon

Left: Slicing fresh tomatoes for lunch in the fields, Lebanon

Above: Grape harvest, Lebanon

73

The Kelly Girls' Tabbouleh

Serves 6 to 8

1 cup (140 g) fine bulgur wheat

5 ripe red tomatoes, cut into dice

2 large bunches fresh flat-leaf or curly parsley, leaves and tender stems, finely chopped

1 cup (50 g) fresh mint leaves, finely chopped, or 1 tablespoon dried

1 bunch green onions, finely chopped

Juice of 3 lemons

¼ cup (60 ml) extra-virgin olive oil, preferably Lebanese unfiltered

Kosher salt and freshly ground black pepper

Lettuce or red or green cabbage leaves, for serving (optional)

This recipe comes from my grandma Ruth, who we called Sitti. Her father's last name was changed from "Khalil" to "Kelly" when he arrived at Ellis Island in 1905, and Sitti and her three sisters were known as the "Kelly girls" their whole lives. Until I was an adult I don't think I'd ever made this tabbouleh for fewer than two hundred people. It was one of Mom's catering staples, and by the time I was a teenager I could whip up enough to serve hordes of hundreds in a matter of minutes.

In this as in most dishes, Mom prefers curly parsley, whose leaves are easy to pluck from the stems; but in Lebanon it's always the flat-leaf, which I prefer for its flavor and texture. The amounts here are the blueprint for our family's tabbouleh, which has a nice balance of everything, but I usually tweak the proportions of the main ingredients based on what time of year it is. When tomatoes are in season I go heavy on them; when they're out of season I go heavier on the parsley; and when nothing is in season, I go heaviest on the bulgur. We adapted this for Compass Rose simply by changing out the bulgur for freekeh; it's delicious that way, too. Aunt Joan added chopped Persian cucumber once and Mom and Aunt Jan were utterly horrified; but I admit that I loved it, so try it if it sounds good to you.

Rinse and drain the bulgur in a fine-mesh strainer and put it in a bowl. Add cold water to cover by 2 inches (5 cm) and let stand until tender, about 30 minutes.

In a large bowl combine the tomatoes, parsley, mint, and green onions.

Drain the bulgur through a fine-mesh strainer, and then squeeze it to release as much of the water as possible.

Add the bulgur to the vegetables along with the lemon juice, oil, 1 teaspoon salt, and ½ teaspoon pepper and mix well. Taste and adjust the seasoning. The tabbouleh can be served at once or covered and refrigerated up to 2 days.

Transfer the tabbouleh to a serving bowl. Serve at once, with lettuce or cabbage leaves, if using, to pick up the salad and create a bite, or a bakoun, as Mom would say (see page 29).

Tomato Cucumber Salad

Serves 6 to 8

4 ripe tomatoes (about 1½ pounds / 680 g), cut in bite-size pieces

8 Persian cucumbers, sliced lengthewise in half and then crosswise into thin half-moons

1 medium onion, thinly sliced lengthwise

¼ cup (60 ml) extra-virgin olive oil, preferably Lebanese unfiltered, or to taste, or ¼ cup (60 ml) Sumac Vinaigrette (recipe follows)

1 tablespoon dried mint

2 teaspoons kosher salt

1 teaspoon freshly ground black pepper

I don't know a country in this region of the world that doesn't have their version of this salad. In Georgia they add walnuts, and that extra crunch and tannic note can be really nice. But this Lebanese one is closest to my heart. We grew cucumbers pretty much entirely so we could eat this salad during the summer.

In a large bowl, place the tomatoes, cucumbers, onion, olive oil, mint, salt, and pepper.

Toss gently until all the vegetables are well coated in oil and mint. Serve.

Sumac Vinaigrette

Makes about 1½ cups (360 ml)

The tomato cucumber salad above that I grew up eating is a beautiful testament to how delicious simplicity can be. Every now and then, though, I want to add a little flair, and I replace the olive oil with this tangy dressing.

***

¾ cup (180 ml) fresh lemon juice (from about 3 lemons)

2 small cloves garlic, minced

1 tablespoon ground sumac

1½ teaspoons honey

Kosher salt

¾ cup (180 ml) extra-virgin olive oil, preferably Lebanese unfiltered

***

In a small bowl, whisk together the lemon juice, garlic, sumac, honey, and a couple pinches of salt.

Whisking constantly, pour in the olive oil in a slow, steady stream. Continue whisking until well blended.

Store in a tightly closed jar in the refrigerator up to 2 weeks. Shake or stir before using.

Fattoush

Summer Salad with Crisped Flatbread

Serves 2

For the lemon-pomegranate dressing:

¼ cup (60 ml) rosé or sherry vinegar

2 tablespoons fresh lemon juice (from about 1 lemon)

2 tablespoons pomegranate molasses

1 tablespoon ground sumac

½ cup (120 ml) grapeseed oil

For the fattoush:

1 cup (180 g) coarsely chopped ripe tomatoes or quartered cherry tomatoes

1 cup (115 g) Persian cucumbers sliced lengthwise in half and then crosswise into ¼-inch (6 mm) half-moons

¼ cup (13 g) fresh mint leaves

¼ cup (13 g) fresh flat-leaf parsley leaves

¼ cup (30 g) Sumac Onions (recipe follows)

1 tablespoon ground sumac

Kosher salt and freshly ground black pepper

3 cups (145 g) chopped gem or other tender lettuce

1 cup (65 g) torn and toasted flatbread (see Note)

Fattoush is commonly known as a "bread salad" but at its core it is truly a summer vegetable salad, and it's at its absolute best when beautifully ripe, in-season tomatoes and cucumbers are used. Although lettuce plays a role, it's not the star of this show. Fattoush should be bold in both flavor and appearance. I like to think of it as a raucous celebration of the height of summer, and this recipe as written here captures that spirit. And still, sometimes I like to turn the dial to eleven and add whatever I have that I think will highlight those tomatoes and cucumbers. If you have a garden of any size, from windowsill to backyard, don't be afraid to throw in any extra fresh herbs. Or, if you're lucky enough that your garden is host to purslane, don't pull and toss it on the compost heap! This weed is worth saving and eating, both for its good nutritional value and for its tang, which plays especially well with the sumac and pomegranate molasses in this salad.

To make the dressing, in a medium bowl whisk together the vinegar, lemon juice, pomegranate molasses, and sumac. Whisking constantly, add the oil in a slow, steady stream. Whisk until very well blended. Set aside until needed.

To make the fattoush, in a large bowl, combine the tomatoes, cucumbers, mint, parsley, sumac onions, sumac, and a pinch each of salt and pepper. Toss gently to combine. Add just enough dressing to lightly coat all of the ingredients and let stand for at least 15 minutes and up to 1 hour.

When ready to serve, add the lettuce and flatbread to the salad and toss until everything is well dispersed. Taste and adjust the seasoning, and serve.

Store leftover dressing in an airtight container in the refrigerator up to 1 month.

Note: To prepare the toasted flatbread, preheat the oven to 375°F (190°C). Tear the bread into bite-size pieces and spread the pieces on a rimmed baking sheet. Toast until lightly browned, stirring once or twice, about 10 minutes. One 6-inch (15 cm) pita yields about 1 cup (65 g) toasted pieces.

Sumac Onions

Makes about 5 cups (1.2 liters)

These tangy onions are a foundational item in Maydān's kitchen. They are a snap to make, they keep for ages, and they are a very welcome burst of flavor and color on so many dishes. Sometimes mixed with fresh herbs (see below), sometimes on their own, they appear on every kebab and most of the meat and fish dishes.

***

3 medium red onions, thinly sliced

1 tablespoon ground sumac

¼ cup (60 ml) distilled white vinegar, or as needed

***

In a large bowl, toss the onions with the sumac until well coated. Transfer them to a 6-cup (1.4 liter) nonreactive container with an airtight lid.

Heat the vinegar in the microwave or on the stovetop until hot. Pour the hot vinegar over the onions. Tightly close the container and shake it a few times to fully coat the onions in vinegar.

Set aside for at least 2 hours before using. Tightly close and refrigerate up to 1 month, giving the container a shake every now and then.

Sumac Onion and Herb Salad

Makes 3½ cups (840 ml)

***

2 cups (480 ml) Sumac Onions (above)

2 cups (480 ml) picked herb leaves, such as parsley and cilantro

***

In a medium bowl combine the sumac onions with the herbs. Toss gently to combine. Use at once.

Patata Salata

Lebanese Potato Salad

Serves 6 to 8

6 medium all-purpose potatoes (2 pounds / 910 g), scrubbed

Kosher salt

1 large onion, thinly sliced lengthwise

1 tablespoon dried mint and/or 6 sprigs fresh mint, leaves chopped, plus a few mint sprigs for serving

¼ cup (60 ml) extra-virgin olive oil, preferably Lebanese unfiltered

Juice of 2 lemons, plus more as needed

Kosher salt and freshly ground black pepper

My mom's potato salad—with fresh and dried mint, Lebanese olive oil, and lots of lemon—is the taste and smell of summer to me. For a long time this was the only kind of potato salad I knew. My lips didn't touch a mayonnaise-based potato salad until I was far past childhood. Even now, when I have had plenty of opportunity to taste the creamy potato salad that is so familiar to most Americans, I still prefer this one by a mile. I like to make a batch of this on the weekend to have in my fridge so I can eat it for any meal, or even between meals, all week.

Place the potatoes in a large pot and cover with cold water by 2 inches (5 cm). Generously salt the water. Cover the pan and bring to a boil over medium-high heat. Reduce the heat to a simmer and cook, partially covered, until the potatoes are tender when pierced with a sharp knife, 15 to 20 minutes. Drain and set aside until cool enough to handle.

Peel the potatoes and cut them into 1-inch (2.5 cm) cubes. Place them in a large bowl.

Add the onion and dried and/or fresh mint to the potatoes and very gently toss the ingredients to combine them.

Add the oil, lemon juice, 1 teaspoon salt, and ½ teaspoon pepper and mix well. Taste and add more lemon juice or salt and pepper as needed. Garnish with fresh mint sprigs, if using.

Serve at room temperature. Store leftovers in an airtight container in the refrigerator for up to 1 week; let come to room temperature (or close) before serving for best flavor.

Refrigerate leftovers in an airtight container up to 4 days.

Salatet Malfouf

Mint Cabbage Salad

Serves 10 to 12

1 cup (240 ml) fresh lemon juice (from about 4 lemons)

¼ cup (9 g) dried mint

1 small head green cabbage (about 1½ pounds / 680 g), quartered, cored, and shredded

1 small head radicchio (4 ounces / 115 g), cored and shredded (optional)

2 teaspoons kosher salt, plus more as needed

¼ cup (60 ml) extra-virgin olive oil, preferably Lebanese unfiltered, plus more for serving

Like the potato in the Patata Salata (Lebanese Potato Salad, page 80), here the cabbage is primarily the medium that lets the lemon, mint, and olive oil do their thing. This salad is very popular at potlucks or picnics because it's refreshing, crunchy, and can stand on its own or go with just about anything. Serve it wherever you'd typically serve a tangy green salad. It might seem funny to use dried mint in a summer salad, but we were usually using mint that my grandmother or aunt had dried themselves (see page 24), and over the years I've realized that I actually prefer dried mint in certain dishes, like this one and the potato salad. Even with store-bought dried mint it's delicious enough that we served it on our very first menu at Maydān (and many menus since then). We opened during the winter, and we wanted to offer a bright salad that was in season but would taste like summer. This fits the bill perfectly.

In a large bowl, combine the lemon juice and mint. Add the cabbage, radicchio (if using), and salt.

Toss with your hands, gently rubbing the cabbage to help soften it a bit. Add the oil and toss to coat.

Cover and chill at least 2 hours and up to 12 hours. Before serving, taste and adjust the salt if necessary and drizzle with a little more olive oil. Serve cold or at cool room temperature.

Hinbe
Wilted Dandelion Greens Salad

Serves 2 to 4

¼ cup (60 ml) extra-virgin olive oil, preferably Lebanese unfiltered

2 bunches dandelion greens (about 1 pound / 455 g total), rinsed well and sliced into 2- to 3-inch / 5- to 7.5-cm lengths

3 cloves garlic, crushed with garlic press

½ teaspoon kosher salt, plus more as needed

Juice of 1 lemon, plus more as needed

1 tablespoon store-bought fried shallots

There were times my dad wouldn't drive more than a few feet past a field of dandelions without hitting the brakes so that we could all pile out of the car to pick the wild greens. Back home, he'd dump our haul into a big old-timey tub we kept outside and turn the garden hose on them. Mom would take over from there. She'd leave them to soak for a bit to remove some of the bitterness and get the dirt out, then she'd drain them well and wilt them in lemon and olive oil. To this day I have to stop myself from impulsively shouting "STOP!" whenever David and I pass a patch of dandelions while whizzing down the interstate. The truth is that these days we're more likely to eat the cultivated dandelion greens from the store than the wild ones. I don't soak the store-bought greens because they're typically less bitter than those greens Mom was working with. Also, sautéing them for several minutes helps to tone down a lot of the bitterness and adding lemon juice and fried shallots brings up great sweet and tangy notes. Don't worry about the long cooking time. Dandelion greens are tough; they can take it.

In a large sauté pan, heat the oil over high heat until very hot but not smoking.

Add as many greens to the pan as will fit, and use tongs to toss and turn them so that there is more room in the pan for the remaining greens. Add the garlic and the salt and sauté until the garlic is fragrant, about 1 minute.

Reduce the heat and cook gently until the stems are tender and the bitterness is tempered, about 15 minutes. Add the lemon juice, increase the heat to high, and cook for another minute.

Remove the pan from the heat and let the greens cool to room temperature. Taste and adjust lemon juice or salt if necessary. Top with the shallots just before serving.

Shakshuka

Serves 4

1 tablespoon extra-virgin olive oil, preferably Lebanese unfiltered

1½ cups (165 g) diced onions

¼ cup (35 g) minced garlic (from about 8 large cloves)

2 cups (330 g) diced peeled (page 105) plum tomatoes or canned peeled plum tomatoes (see Note)

4 cups (600 g) diced drained jarred piquillo peppers

1 tablespoon ground turmeric

1 tablespoon sweet paprika

1½ teaspoons cumin seeds, toasted (see page 39) and ground

2½ tablespoons Harissa (page 35)

1½ tablespoons minced fresh flat-leaf parsley, plus chopped parsley for garnish

1 tablespoon minced fresh thyme

1 teaspoon kosher salt

½ teaspoon freshly ground black pepper

4 large eggs

¼ cup (40 g) crumbled feta

Zhough (page 37), for serving

Labne or plain full-fat yogurt, for serving

Grilled or toasted bread, for serving

When we first put this beloved pepper-and-tomato skillet dish on the menu at Compass Rose, we quickly learned that many countries and people, including those from Israel, Tunisia, Morocco, Yemen, and Palestine, all claim it as their own.

This is why now we say simply that shakshuka hails from the Middle East and North Africa, like so many other lip-smacking dishes. Here, soft-cooked eggs are nestled in a deeply spiced base of peppers, tomatoes, and onions. And our shakshuka has an additional flourish that I believe makes it the best I've had—it's topped with salty feta, herby zhough, and tangy, creamy labne. Shakshuka begs to be served with a small mountain of toasted bread so that every last bit of sauce and egg yolk can be soaked up.

Preheat the oven to 375°F (190°C).

In a nonreactive ovenproof sauté pan or skillet, heat the olive oil over medium heat until hot. Add the onions and cook until lightly browned, about 10 minutes. Add the garlic and sauté until fragrant, about 2 minutes. Stir in the tomatoes and cook until the liquid has cooked out of them, 4 to 5 minutes. Add the piquillos, lower the heat to medium-low, and cook until reduced and thickened, about 15 minutes.

Stir in the turmeric, paprika, and cumin and cook for 1 minute. Stir in the harissa and cook for 1 minute. Stir in the parsley, thyme, salt, and pepper. Taste and adjust the seasoning with more salt or pepper.

With the back of a spoon make 4 shallow divots in the surface of the mixture. Crack an egg into each divot. Sprinkle with the feta.

Bake until the egg whites are opaque but the yolks still wiggle when the pan is tapped or moved, 8 to 10 minutes; note that the eggs will keep cooking a bit after they are removed from the oven.

Dollop with spoonfuls of zhough and labne and sprinkle chopped parsley on top. Serve at once, directly from the pan, with lots of grilled or toasted bread.

Note: For best flavor, buy whole tomatoes in the can and chop them yourself rather than buying already-diced tomatoes in the can.

Badrijani Nigvzit

Georgian Eggplant Rolls
with Walnut Filling

Makes 16 to 18 rolls; serves 4 to 6

2 cups (240 g) walnuts

3 cloves garlic, chopped

1 teaspoon dried blue fenugreek

1 teaspoon ground coriander

1 teaspoon sweet paprika

1 teaspoon ground dried marigold flower
(optional, see Note)

1 teaspoon kosher salt, plus more as needed

3 tablespoons white wine vinegar

½ cup (120 ml) grapeseed or other neutral
vegetable oil, or as needed

2 eggplant (about 2 pounds / 910 g total),
sliced lengthwise ¼ inch (6 mm) thick

Pomegranate seeds, for garnish

Here walnuts are transformed into a tangy, tasty spread that is rolled into pan-fried slices of eggplant. The result is a vibrant contrast of crunchy-creamy textures and tangy-sweet flavors. From the first time I tasted these in Moscow, where they were prepared by a lovely Georgian woman, I haven't stopped thinking about them. I'm almost always looking forward to my next opportunity to eat them, which is why I'm grateful that my dear Georgian friend Mamuka Tsereteli shared this easy recipe. Mamuka is a professor, wine importer, and the unofficial cultural ambassador of Georgia in DC, and I feel lucky to call him my friend.

Place the walnuts and garlic in a food processor and process until finely chopped.

Transfer to a medium bowl and add the blue fenugreek, coriander, paprika, marigold (if using), the salt, vinegar, and 3 tablespoons water. Stir until well blended and moist enough to stick together when squeezed between your fingers; add water 1 teaspoon at a time if the mixture is too dry. Set aside.

Line a baking sheet with several layers of paper towels and set next to the stovetop.

Heat 2 tablespoons of the oil in a large skillet over medium-high heat until it shimmers. Add the eggplant slices in a single layer (do this in batches) and fry until lightly browned on both sides, about 2 minutes per side.

Transfer the slices to the paper towels and blot the top with more paper towels to soak up excess oil. Lightly season with salt. Continue with the remaining eggplant slices, adding more oil to the pan as necessary.

Spoon 1 to 2 teaspoons walnut mixture at the narrowest end of 1 eggplant slice. Roll up the slice to enclose the filling and place on a serving platter. Repeat with the remaining eggplant slices and walnut filling.

Garnish with pomegranate seeds. Serve at room temperature.

Note: Ground dried marigold flower has a sweet, floral taste and aroma. It is sometimes called Imeretian saffron after the province of Imereti, and it may even be labeled simply "saffron" if the producer is Georgian.

Maydān's Grilled Carrots with Harissa

Serves 4

Kosher salt

1½ pounds (680 g) carrots, preferably all roughly the same thickness, peeled, if desired

Extra-virgin olive oil, preferably Lebanese unfiltered

Juice of ½ lemon

¼ cup (60 ml) Harissa (page 35)

Flaky sea salt (such as Maldon), for garnish

Chopped chives, for garnish

When we were developing the menu for Maydān, we wanted some vegetables that could really hold up to the fire for our vegetarian and vegan audience, and carrots were always high on our list of possibilities. At bars in Lebanon, a small dish of carrots soaking in fresh lemon juice is often served along with your drink. They are about as far from beer nuts as you can get, and still they absolutely deliver the crunch, tang, and sweetness of the best bar snacks. Add some smoke and heat and you've got a home run (when in a bar, sports metaphors work best), and that's exactly what this dish is. The carrots' natural sweetness is amplified when steamed and grilled, and the tart lemon counteracts the spice of the harissa and the char on the carrot. If you're worried that not everyone will love the spiciness, serve the harissa on the side. One insider tip that I must share is that we like to put these carrots on the table at the same time as the cheesy, nutty, honeyed halloumi with dukkah (page 232) because the mix of flavors and textures is out of this world.

Prepare a hot grill.

Meanwhile, in a pot with a steamer insert or in a covered sauté pan fitted with an expandable steamer basket, add water to a depth of 2 inches (5 cm) and a couple generous pinches of kosher salt. Bring the water to a boil. Add the carrots to the steamer insert or basket, cover, and steam until they're just shy of being al dente, or tender but firm to the bite, about 20 minutes.

Transfer the carrots to a rimmed baking sheet or platter. Drizzle with a bit of oil and salt them lightly.

Grill the carrots, turning them a few times, until lightly browned on all sides. Transfer them to a serving platter.

Squeeze the lemon juice over the carrots. Drizzle the harissa back and forth across the carrots—this is easiest to do if the harissa is in a squeeze bottle or piping bag. (Alternatively, put the harissa in a small dish to pass alongside the carrots.) Sprinkle with flaky salt and chives, and serve.

Potato Kibbeh

Serves 8 to 10

1½ cups (210 g) fine bulgur

3 pounds (1.4 kg) all-purpose potatoes, peeled and cut into 2-inch (5 cm) pieces (see Note)

Kosher salt

1 tablespoon dried marjoram

½ cup (20 g) finely chopped fresh basil

1 bunch spring onions, white and green parts, finely chopped

1 teaspoon dried parsley

¾ teaspoon ground white pepper

Extra-virgin olive oil, preferably Lebanese unfiltered

The term *kibbeh* is used broadly to refer to a dish in which meat or potato or another vegetable is mixed with bulgur; from there it can be baked, fried, or served as is. The defining characteristic of kibbeh is that bulgur; I've never known a kibbeh without it. When I was growing up, what we called potato kibbeh was a lot like a shepherd's pie, with layers of potato and seasoned ground lamb baked in a casserole dish; except during Lent, when the lamb was omitted and the potato and bulgur alone were still substantial enough to fill everyone up. Then I went to Lebanon and tasted this kind of kibbeh, which is much more like a vegetarian rendition of the beloved raw lamb dish called kibbeh nayeh (page 196), and I love it. Fine bulgur adds nubbly texture to the mashed potatoes, and abundant fresh and dried herbs and green onions give it a bit of crunch and a lot of savory flavor.

Place the bulgur in a medium bowl and add cold water to cover by about 2 inches (5 cm). Let stand for 30 minutes. Drain thoroughly in a fine-mesh strainer.

Meanwhile, place the potatoes in a large saucepan. Add cold water to cover by 1 inch (2.5 cm) and a couple generous pinches of salt.

Bring to a boil over medium-high heat. Reduce the heat and simmer until tender, 10 to 12 minutes.

Drain the potatoes and place them in a large bowl. Use a potato masher to mash the potatoes while they are still hot.

Add the drained bulgur to the bowl with the potatoes.

Add the marjoram, basil, spring onions, parsley, white pepper, ½ teaspoon salt, and ¼ cup (60 ml) olive oil. Use your hands to knead the mixture together until well combined; add more olive oil if the texture is too dry.

Transfer to a shallow serving bowl. Use the back of a spoon to make a shallow divot in the surface and drizzle some olive oil on top. Serve.

Note: For a fun and colorful alternative, substitute an equal weight of peeled and seeded pumpkin for the potatoes. Coat the pumpkin lightly with olive oil, season with salt, and roast in a 400°F (205°C) oven until soft, 25 to 30 minutes. Proceed as directed.

Batata Harra
Lebanese Spicy Potatoes

Serves 6 to 8

3 pounds (1.4 kg) Yukon Gold or all-purpose potatoes (about 8 medium), peeled and cubed

3 tablespoons extra-virgin olive oil, preferably Lebanese unfiltered

1½ teaspoons kosher salt, plus more as needed

1 teaspoon sweet paprika

4 cloves garlic, finely chopped

1 teaspoon red pepper flakes, or to taste

1 cup (40 g) chopped fresh cilantro

Juice of ½ lemon, plus more as needed

½ teaspoon freshly ground black pepper

Crisp roasted potatoes tossed with sautéed garlic, crushed red pepper, and lots of fresh cilantro and lemon juice burst with flavor. I'm a firm believer that potatoes should always be available on the table if it's possible. I think people often assume that rice will be served instead of potatoes alongside meat dishes like kebabs (pages 167–187), but actually batata harra is usually on that table, too. I'm not really an either/or kind of person when it comes to delicious carbohydrates. If you're ever stuck in a rice-or-potatoes moment, remember that you can always go with both!

Preheat the oven to 450°F (230°C). Line two rimmed baking sheets with parchment paper or use ungreased baking sheets.

In a large bowl, toss the potatoes with 2 tablespoons olive oil, 1 teaspoon salt, and the paprika. Spread the potatoes on the lined baking sheets. Roast until tender and nicely browned, 30 to 35 minutes, flipping once or twice.

Toward the end of roasting, heat the remaining tablespoon olive oil in a medium skillet over medium heat. Add the garlic and cook until lightly browned, 1 to 2 minutes. Stir in the red pepper flakes.

Transfer the roasted potatoes to a large bowl. Add the cilantro, lemon juice, pepper, remaining salt, and the garlic and red pepper flakes. Toss until well coated. Taste and add more lemon juice or salt if necessary. Serve hot.

Slow-Grilled Cauliflower with Tahina and Zhough

Serves 4 as a main dish,
6 to 8 as a side

1 cup grapeseed oil, plus more for grilling

1 tablespoon kosher salt

1 tablespoon ground turmeric

2 teaspoons nigella seeds

2 teaspoons ground coriander

2 medium to large heads cauliflower
(2 to 2½ pounds / 910 g to 1.2 kg each),
leaves and stems trimmed

1 cup (240 ml) Tahina (page 34), plus more
for serving

1 cup (240 ml) Zhough (page 37), plus more
for serving

1 cup (240 ml) Sumac Onions (page 79),
plus more for serving

Flaky sea salt (such as Maldon), for garnish

½ cup (20 g) loosely packed mixed fresh herb
leaves (such as cilantro, parsley, and mint)

Equipment: Smoking wood chunks, such as
oak or apple (optional)

I have nothing against the cauliflower "steaks" that at one point seemed to be the only alternative offered to vegetarians at restaurants across the nation. But at Maydān we wondered why anyone would stop at a slice of cauliflower when you could have the whole damn head? The chefs hang the marinated heads above the fire at the restaurant to slowly cook them. At home we get the smoky, roasty effect by grill-roasting them over indirect heat. Served with bright sauces and our tangy-sweet sumac onions and fresh herbs, it's a hearty main dish for up to four people or a side for more. But please don't hesitate to prepare this if you're only feeding one or two people; it keeps beautifully in the refrigerator up to a week.

In a large bowl, whisk together the oil, salt, turmeric, nigella seeds, and coriander. Add the cauliflower and gently turn until thoroughly coated. Let stand at room temperature 1 hour.

Meanwhile, prepare a hot, two-zone fire in a charcoal grill with a lid: Light a hot fire. When the coals are covered with gray ash, rake them to one side of the grill, creating a cooler zone on the other side to use for indirect cooking. Put a couple chunks of smoking wood, if using, on top of the coals. Lightly grease the top grate with oil and put it in place.

Place the cauliflower on the oiled grate over the side without coals, reserving any marinade. Cover the grill, arranging the lid so that the vent is directly over the cauliflower; open the vent. Grill, covered, until the cauliflower is tender and a skewer slides into the center with just a little resistance, about 1 hour to 1 hour 15 minutes, brushing with any reserved marinade and rotating 180 degrees halfway through cook time. Add more charcoal to the fire as necessary to keep it hot and add smoking chunks, if using, to keep the smoke going.

Transfer the cauliflower to the grate directly over the coals; grill, uncovered, turning occasionally, until golden brown and lightly charred, 5 to 10 minutes.

Place the cauliflower heads on a serving platter. Drizzle the tahina and zhough over the cauliflower heads and top with the sumac onions. Sprinkle with flaky salt and herb leaves. Serve with bowls of tahina, zhough, and sumac onions.

Mchicha Wanazi
Spinach in Coconut Milk

Serves 8

6 tablespoons (90 ml) extra-virgin olive oil, preferably Lebanese unfiltered

1¾ pounds (800 g) fresh spinach, rinsed well

4 teaspoons kosher salt

2 large red bell peppers, cored and thinly sliced

1 large green bell pepper, cored and thinly sliced

1 serrano pepper, seeded and thinly sliced

3 shallots, sliced (about 2 cups / 230 g)

2½-inch (6 cm) piece fresh ginger, peeled and thinly sliced into coins or finely chopped

4 cloves garlic, sliced

4 cans (13½ ounces / 400 ml each) coconut milk, preferably Chaokoh brand

2 teaspoons freshly grated nutmeg

Pita bread, for serving

Zanzibar is a big part of Omani history, as we learned firsthand when we traveled to Oman and were invited to cook with a family that owns a very well-known Zanzibari restaurant there. The provenance of so many dishes from this part of the world can be hard to pin down definitively. This dish is an exception, and its origin story is eye-opening. For roughly 150 years, until the middle of the nineteenth century, Zanzibar, off the coast of East Africa, was the capital of the sultanate of Oman, almost 2,500 miles (4,000 kilometers) away. This might help explain how coconuts found their way into Omani cuisine—today Oman palms are the biggest producers of the fruit in the Gulf region—and why it was in Oman that we learned how to prepare this wonderfully creamy, aromatic stew of fresh spinach, bell and serrano peppers, and sweet shallots bathed in coconut milk laced with fresh ginger, garlic, and nutmeg. Serve with plenty of pita or other flatbread to help wipe the bowls clean.

In a large Dutch oven, heat 2 tablespoons of the oil over medium heat. Add the spinach and a few pinches of the salt. Cook, using tongs to toss the spinach, until wilted. Transfer the spinach to a strainer to remove excess liquid. When cool enough to handle, chop the spinach and set aside.

Return the Dutch oven to medium heat. Add 2 tablespoons of the oil to the pan. Add the bell peppers and serrano pepper and cook, stirring until the peppers are softened but still have some bite (they'll cook a bit more at the end, so you don't want them to be too soft now). Transfer to a bowl and return the Dutch oven to the heat.

Heat the remaining 2 tablespoons oil in the pan. Add the shallots, ginger, and garlic and sauté until translucent, about 5 minutes. Add the coconut milk and bring to a simmer, stirring and scraping the bottom of the pan to deglaze.

Add the nutmeg along with the cooked spinach and peppers. Bring to a simmer for 2 to 3 minutes, until the stew is thick enough to coat the back of a spoon but loose enough that it wouldn't stay put on a chip. Serve with pita bread.

Left: Learning to make Mchicha Wanazi, Oman

Stuffed Grape Leaves

Makes about 40 dolmas;
serves 8 to 10

40 to 50 fresh or jarred grape leaves that are roughly the size of your hand, plus a few extra for the pot (see Note)

1½ pounds (680 g) coarse ground lamb (optional)

1 cup (185 g) uncooked white rice, such as Ben's Original, or a medium-grain rice such as Arborio or Egyptian (use 3 cups / 555 g if omitting the lamb)

1 tablespoon kosher salt

1 teaspoon freshly ground black pepper

Juice of 2 lemons

3 lemons, sliced, for cooking the dolmas

Extra-virgin olive oil, preferably Lebanese unfiltered, for the pot

Labne, for serving (optional)

Fresh grape leaves are abundant in the wilds of suburbia. Many a home gardener will rip them out without realizing how tasty those leaves could be with a bit of soaking and stuffing. I remember vividly the day we stopped at the cemetery in Michigan where my grandparents are buried and my mother quickly grew distracted by the lush grape vines growing along a fence near Sitti and Giddo's gravestones. Mom was certain that Sitti was sending us a sign, apparently to make this dish, because that's what we did with those cemetery grape leaves.

The lamb here is optional, though in my family dolmas always contain meat; we seem to have an aversion to meat-free things.

If using fresh grape leaves, snip off and discard the stems, rinse them well, and place in a large bowl. Cover with boiling water and let stand 15 minutes, until softened. Drain thoroughly. If using jarred grape leaves, rinse and thoroughly drain them. Set aside any grape leaves that are torn or too small to stuff.

In a large bowl, combine the lamb (if using), rice, salt, pepper, and the juice of 1 lemon. Stir to mix the ingredients together. Have ready a baking sheet or platter to hold the stuffed grape leaves.

Lay 1 grape leaf shiny side down on the work surface with the broad base of the leaf closest to you. Place about 1 tablespoon of the meat and rice mixture across the bottom of the leaf.

Fold the bottom of the leaf up to cover the filling. Fold in both sides, then roll all the way up; the roll should be snug but not too tight, as you want to leave room for the rice to expand as it cooks. Continue filling and rolling the grape leaves until all of the filling is used.

Oil the bottom and sides of a large Dutch oven or other pot with a lid. Line the bottom of the pan with grape leaves to cover it completely and arrange half of the lemon slices on top; these will keep the dolmas from scorching during cooking.

Place the stuffed grape leaves seam side down in the pan, arranging them in even layers, and alternating the direction of each layer. When all the dolmas are in the pot, arrange the remaining lemon slices on top. Place an inverted plate on top to hold down the rolls.

Add water to cover and squeeze in the juice of the remaining lemon. Bring to a gentle boil over medium heat. Cover the pan with the lid, reduce the heat to low, and cook until the rice is tender, 45 to 60 minutes.

Using tongs, carefully remove the plate, then remove and discard the lemon slices. Transfer the stuffed grape leaves to a baking sheet lined with a kitchen towel.

Serve hot or warm, with a side of labne, if desired.

Koosa

*Stuffed Summer Squash
with Lamb and Rice*

Serves 6 to 8

12 to 18 green summer squash (koosa),
each approximately 5 inches (12 cm) long

2 pounds (910 g) coarsely ground lamb
(optional)

1 cup (185 g) uncooked white rice, such as
Ben's Original, or a medium-grain rice such
as Arborio or Egyptian (use 3 cups / 555 g if
omitting the lamb)

¼ cup (½ stick / 115 g) unsalted butter, melted

2 tablespoons ground cinnamon

2 teaspoons kosher salt

1 teaspoon freshly ground black pepper

¼ cup (60 ml) extra-virgin olive oil, preferably
Lebanese unfiltered, or vegetable oil

1 medium onion, diced or thinly sliced

1 quart (960 ml) Open-Kettle Tomatoes
(recipe follows) or 1 can (28 ounces / 794 g)
whole peeled tomatoes

Handful fresh spearmint leaves or ⅓ cup (12 g)
dried mint

In Arabic, the word *mashi* means "to stuff," and we really like to stuff things! Don't fret if you're game to try this filling, or the one on the previous page, but neither grape leaves nor koosa strike your fancy. You can use these fillings to stuff all sorts of items that might be hanging out in your refrigerator crisper: mushrooms, eggplant, peppers, cabbage leaves, you name it.

As far back as I can recall, it has been the rule in my family that we preserve summer tomatoes and squash specifically so that we can have this dish at Christmas. These days I'll still sometimes preserve summer tomatoes to use year-round (see page 105), as they really do have far superior flavor to even the very best store-bought canned tomatoes, but I tend to depend on my local markets for the squash. The best squash for koosa are shorter and squatter and a lighter shade of green than standard zucchini; they are sometimes labeled as *koosa* or *kousa*, but not reliably. I've had the best luck finding them at Asian markets. Once you have the koosa in hand, you can use a butter knife and small spoon, as I do, to core them, although I know some people swear by special zucchini corers available online and at kitchen-supply stores.

As with most dishes that involve optional lamb, my mother only ever includes the meat, a position her sisters generally agree with. But if you want to enjoy your Christmas dinner, I recommend that you not ask about the cinnamon. Don't get me wrong, it is extremely tasty, and everyone agrees that it must go in the meat stuffing. The problems arise—and I assure you, arise they do—when one asks whether or not to put cinnamon in the tomatoes as well. Where some might see a simple difference of opinion, others recognize that taking a stand on either side is akin to a declaration of war on whomever has taken a divergent position.

Believe me when I say that I truly do not wish to ruffle a single of my family's many feathers, but I take seriously my role as author of this collection of recipes and as such I can't simply walk away from the debate without picking a side, alas. So I'll say first that the cinnamon is delicious no matter how it shows up in this dish, and all of us do at least agree that 2 tablespoons is a perfect amount for these proportions. But if you're uneasy, add a lesser amount first and taste as you go. Any amount is very good. (Also, I only put the cinnamon in the meat stuffing, but you definitely did not hear that from me if anyone asks.)

[recipe continues]

To prepare the koosa for stuffing, wash them gently with a vegetable brush. Working with 1 koosa at a time, slice off the stem. Using a zucchini corer or butter (table) knife, scoop out the flesh, leaving a ¼-inch-thick (6 mm) shell, taking care not to poke through the skin. Rinse to make sure that all the loose particles are out. Continue with all of the koosa.

In a large bowl, place the lamb, if using, rice, melted butter, cinnamon, 1 teaspoon salt, and ½ teaspoon pepper. Use your hands to mix until well combined.

Stuff the lamb mixture into each koosa; make sure to push the filling all the way to the bottom of the hole you scooped out, do not pack too tightly to leave room for the rice to expand. If there is any filling left over, use it to stuff whatever else you can find in your crisper drawer—mushroom caps, bell peppers, eggplant, almost anything can be stuffed—or, if there is meat in the filling, roll it into little meatballs to cook in the pot with the koosa, or reserve them for another use.

In an 8- to 10-quart (7.5 to 9.4 liter) pot, heat the oil over medium heat until it shimmers. Add the onion and a pinch of salt and pepper and cook until softened and translucent, about 8 minutes.

Add the tomatoes to the pan, breaking them up with your hands as you add them if necessary. Pour a little water in the can or jar and swish it around, then add it to the pot. Add the mint and the remaining teaspoon salt and ½ teaspoon pepper. Bring to a simmer over medium heat and simmer, uncovered, for 15 minutes to let the flavors meld.

Put the stuffed koosa and any extra meatballs in the pan with the tomatoes. Add enough water to cover the koosa. Bring to a gentle boil over medium heat. Cover the pan and cook at a gentle boil until the rice is cooked and the koosa are tender, 45 to 50 minutes.

Serve the koosa with the tomato broth spooned over.

Open-Kettle Tomatoes

Makes about 5 (1-quart / 960-ml) jars

Perfect for koosa or to make Italian tomato sauce, or anywhere you would typically use whole tomatoes or canned San Marzanos. If a recipe calls for tomato *sauce*, however, these won't work. Fresh basil and/or oregano can be added to each jar if desired.

***

13 to 15 pounds (5.9 to 6.8 kg) ripe plum tomatoes, cored

3 tablespoons kosher salt (optional)

5 sprigs fresh basil or fresh oregano (optional)

Equipment: Canning pot, approximately 5 (1-quart / 960-ml) canning jars, lids, and rims; canning tongs or long-handled tongs; large funnel

***

To peel the tomatoes, fill a large saucepan with water and bring it to a boil; reduce the heat to keep the water at a simmer. Place a bowl of ice water next to the stove. Place 6 or more tomatoes in the hot water at once and simmer for about 30 seconds. Use a spider or slotted spoon to transfer the tomatoes to the ice water until cool enough to handle. Use a paring knife to help you remove the tomato skin, starting at the cut where the core was. The skin should come off easily; if it does not, place the tomato back in the simmering water.

Quarter the peeled tomatoes and transfer them to a large nonreactive pot. Add the salt, if using.

Bring the tomatoes to a boil over medium-high heat. When foam forms on the top, skim it off and discard. Turn down heat to a simmer for 45 minutes to 1 hour, until the juices have cooked down a bit, stirring often to prevent sticking on the bottom of the pot.

Meanwhile, sterilize the cans and wash the lids and rings as described below.

When the tomatoes are ready, keep them over the heat as you fill the jars; they need to be hot when they go into the jar.

Work quickly with one jar at a time so the jars stay hot.

Put a sprig of basil or oregano, if using, in the jar. Place the funnel in the jar and ladle in tomatoes, filling up to the neck but leaving at least 1 inch (2.5 cm) from the top of the jar. Wipe off the top rim of the jar with a clean, damp cloth. Place a lid on top of the hot jar and tighten a rim around it. Continue to fill all the jars this way until all of the tomatoes are used.

Place the jars in a draft-free area to cool for 24 to 36 hours. You will usually hear pinging as the lids seal. Before storing the jars, check the seal on each one: Remove the rim and pick up the jar by just the sealed lid; it should hold tight. Additionally, the lid should appear inverted. If it can be pressed down and pops back up, it is not sealed.

Store any unsealed jars in the refrigerator and use within 4 days. Store the sealed jars in a cool, dry place up to 1 year.

Sterilizing Jars for Canning

To sterilize jars for canning, run them through a full regular cycle in the dishwasher. Leave the jars in the hot dishwasher until you are ready to fill them, or stand the clean, dry jars upright on a rack in an oven preheated to 250°F (120°C).

Alternatively, bring a large pot of water to a boil. Carefully place the jars in the water on their sides so they are both filled and surrounded by water. Boil for 5 minutes, then remove the pan from the heat. Leave the jars in the hot water until ready to fill.

Wash the lids and rings in warm, soapy water and let air-dry.

When ready to fill, set a rimmed baking sheet lined with a kitchen towel next to the stovetop. Remove the jars from the dishwasher, oven, or pot of water; use jar tongs or long-handled tongs to carefully remove one jar at a time from the water, making sure to drain all of the water out of it. Place the jars upright on the lined baking sheet.

Lobio Mtsvanilit

Georgian Herbed Kidney Beans

Serves 6 to 8

1 pound (455 g) dried red kidney or other beans (see Note)

¼ cup (60 ml) grapeseed or other neutral vegetable oil

1 large onion, finely chopped

6 cloves garlic, thinly sliced

2 tablespoons ground blue fenugreek or 2 teaspoons ground fenugreek

2 teaspoons Aleppo pepper flakes or ground ancho chile

2 teaspoons ground coriander

2 teaspoons kosher salt, plus more as needed

1 cup (40 g) chopped fresh cilantro, leaves and tender stems, plus more for garnish

½ cup (25 g) chopped fresh dill leaves, plus more for garnish

½ cup (25 g) chopped fresh mint leaves, plus more for garnish

Cornbread or flatbread, for serving (optional)

David and I were in Russia the first time we had beans cooked the Georgian way, with plenty of blue fenugreek and fresh herbs. I will always associate the aroma from a bowl of these beans with the warmth and hospitality of the Georgian people. The beans are served as part of every supra (see page 164), usually with a slightly dry Georgian corn flatbread called mchadi. The beans themselves are delicious, but I confess that I prefer to eat them with the kind of cornbread we make and buy in the U.S. (sweetened or unsweetened—whichever you prefer will work well here), because it soaks up more of the fragrant broth and is frankly just tastier in my opinion. For the best flavor and texture, I do truly recommend starting with dried beans, but don't hesitate to use cans if it means you'll try this sooner! This hearty stew is great for vegetarians and meat-eaters alike.

Rinse and drain the beans and place in a large pot. Add 2 quarts (1.9 liters) water and soak for 24 hours. (It's fine to skip this step; the beans will simply take longer to cook—perhaps twice as long.)

In a large Dutch oven or other large pot with a lid, heat the oil over medium heat until it shimmers. Add the onion and garlic and cook until very soft and lightly brown, about 8 minutes.

Stir in the fenugreek, Aleppo pepper, and coriander and cook until fragrant, about 30 seconds.

Drain the beans and add them to the pot with 2 quarts (1.9 liters) water. Bring to a boil over medium-high heat and boil gently for 10 minutes.

Reduce the heat and simmer, partially covered, until the beans are softened and fully cooked, 1 to 3 hours, depending on the age of the beans; add more water if necessary to keep the beans just covered with liquid. Stir in the salt (it's also fine to stir in the salt once the beans are about three-quarters cooked).

Use a large fork or masher to mash about half the beans, adding water if needed to make the mixture very creamy but not soupy. Turn off the heat and stir in the cilantro, dill, and mint. Taste and add more salt if needed. Cover to keep warm. Serve hot, garnished with cilantro, dill, and mint, and with cornbread, if desired.

Note: You can replace the dried beans here with four 15-ounce (425-g) cans of beans with their liquid. Add the beans with their liquid to the pot at the same point above that you'd add the soaked and drained beans. Cook until the beans are warmed through, about 5 minutes, then continue with mashing the beans. Taste before adding any salt, as you may not need all of what is listed here.

Green Beans with Cinnamon Tomato Sauce

Serves 4 to 6

3 tablespoons extra-virgin olive oil, preferably Lebanese unfiltered, or grapeseed oil

1 medium onion, thinly sliced lengthwise

1 teaspoon kosher salt

½ teaspoon freshly ground black pepper

2 pounds (910 g) green beans, trimmed and cut in half

1 can (28 ounces / 794 g) tomato sauce

1 to 1½ teaspoons ground cinnamon

Sitti's Syrian Rice (page 144, made with or without lamb)

This is, to me, the ultimate comfort food. I don't think anything makes me happier than these green beans served over Sitti's rice. And together they are the perfect accompaniments to Kibbeh Sanieh (page 199). This basic recipe can be adapted a few different ways as noted in the variations, below, to suit many tastes or needs. It can be served with or without lamb or with eggplant in place of the green beans; all are extremely tasty and very satisfying.

In a Dutch oven or other broad, deep pan with a lid, heat the oil over medium heat until it shimmers. Add the onion and a pinch of the salt and pepper and cook until softened and translucent, about 8 minutes.

Add the beans, tomato sauce, cinnamon, the remaining salt and pepper, and enough water to cover the beans. Cover the pan and bring to a boil over medium heat.

Lower the heat and simmer until the beans are tender, 30 to 45 minutes. Serve over rice.

Green Beans with Cinnamon Tomato Sauce and Lamb

Prepare the green beans with cinnamon tomato sauce, browning 1 pound (455 g) boneless lamb leg or loin, cut into 1-inch (2.5 cm) cubes, in the oil with the onions.

Eggplant with Cinnamon Tomato Sauce

Prepare the green beans with cinnamon tomato sauce, replacing the green beans with 2 medium eggplant (3 to 4 pounds / 1.4 to 1.8 kg total), peeled and cut into 1-inch (2.5 cm) cubes.

Top to bottom: Sitti's Syrian Rice (page 144) and
Green Beans with Cinnamon Tomato Sauce (opposite)

Ta'ameya

Falafel

Serves 6 to 8

1⅔ cups (250 g) dried split fava beans

½ cup (60 g) chopped onion

3 cloves (15 g) garlic, chopped

2 cups (50 g) fresh parsley leaves and tender stems, chopped

2 cups (50 g) fresh cilantro leaves and tender stems, chopped

2 teaspoons kosher salt

1 teaspoon ground coriander

Vegetable oil, for deep-frying

3 tablespoons (30 g) white sesame seeds

For serving (all optional except the tahina):
Tahina (page 34)

Pita bread halves

Hummus (page 51)

Shredded cabbage

Sliced tomatoes

Mouneh (page 62) or store-bought pickles

Lemon, cut into wedges

My first encounter with the glory known as make-your-own falafel bars was during some very late nights in Amsterdam during college, and it's possible that every encounter I've had with falafel since then has been measured against this original, frankly unmatchable experience, when I was presented with a pita full of falafel and more toppings and fillings than I could ever fit into one sandwich. Unfortunately most of the falafel I had after that was pretty ordinary, until I was introduced to these. I'd never had falafel made from fava beans until Chef Omar Hegazi joined our team to open Kirby Club in Virginia. Omar is originally from Egypt, where fava is more common in falafel than the chickpeas that Americans are more used to. The other flourish that comes from these falafels' Egyptian roots is the quick dip into sesame seeds that each one gets before being fried.

These make a great light lunch or snack when they are served just with tahina. Or if you want a heartier meal, you can serve with hummus and all the makings to turn them into full pita sandwiches. There's no wrong way to enjoy these!

Place the fava beans in a large bowl and cover with water by 3 inches (7.5 cm). Soak for 12 hours.

Drain the favas and transfer to a food processor. Add the onion, garlic, parsley, cilantro, salt, and coriander. Process until loose and smooth, like the consistency of pancake batter.

Pour the vegetable oil into a deep heavy pot (make sure the level of the oil comes no less than 3 inches (7.5 cm) from the top rim of the pot). Heat the oil to 350°F (175°C) according to a deep-fry thermometer.

Meanwhile, set a baking sheet lined with paper towels near the stovetop.

Using a small dough scoop (about ½ ounce / 15 ml), scoop up the fava mixture. Generously sprinkle the exposed batter in the scoop with sesame seeds. Drop the coated ta'ameya carefully in the hot oil. Cook for 3 minutes, or until golden brown. You can cook a few ta'ameya at a time, but don't crowd the pan.

Use a spider or slotted spoon to transfer the cooked ta'ameya to the paper towels. Continue with the remaining batter and sesame seeds. Adjust the heat as necessary to keep the oil at 350°F (175°C).

Serve with tahina for dipping. Or serve as a "make your own falafel" bar, the way I loved them in Amsterdam: Set out a bowl of the falafel along with a platter of halved pita breads and bowls or plates of tahina, hummus, shredded cabbage, sliced tomatoes, pickles, and lemon wedges and invite everyone to make their own sandwiches.

Empty Quarter

Juicy Carrot Cocktail

Makes 1 cocktail; carrot-apricot base makes enough for about 8 cocktails

For the carrot-apricot base:

8 ounces (240 ml) carrot juice (from 8 to 10 medium carrots)

8 ounces (240 ml) apricot liqueur, such as Bitter Truth

1⅓ ounces (40 ml) Simple Syrup (see recipe at right)

For one cocktail:

Ice, for shaking

2 ounces (60 ml) tequila, such as Pueblo Viejo

2 ounces (60 ml) carrot-apricot base

¾ ounce (22.5 ml) fresh lime juice

Black Lime Salt (see recipe at right), for garnish

Equipment: Coupe glass

When all else fails, this tasty cocktail is a surefire way to get your vegetables.

To make the carrot-apricot base, combine the carrot juice, apricot liqueur, and simple syrup in a bottle or jar with a lid. Cover and shake to combine. Refrigerate up to 1 week.

To make a cocktail, fill a cocktail shaker with ice. Pour in the tequila, carrot-apricot base, and lime juice. Shake vigorously until the outside of the shaker is uncomfortably cold.

Strain into a coupe glass. Sprinkle black lime salt on top and serve.

Simple Syrup

Makes 16 ounces (480 ml)

***

2 cups (400 g) sugar

***

In a medium saucepan, combine the sugar and 2 cups (480 ml) water.

Bring to a gentle boil over medium-high heat, stirring with a wooden spoon until the sugar is dissolved.

Remove the pan from the heat and let cool.

Transfer to a jar and store in the refrigerator up to 2 weeks.

Black Lime Salt

Makes about ⅓ cup (45 g)

***

2 tablespoons ground dried black lime (see page 183)

¼ cup (35 g) flaky sea salt (such as Maldon)

1 tablespoon sugar

***

In a skillet over medium heat, lightly toast the dried black lime until fragrant, about 1 minute.

Transfer to a small bowl. Add the flaky salt and sugar and use a fork to stir until well blended. Spread the mixture on a rimmed baking sheet and let dry out at room temperature for 2 hours.

Store in an airtight container at room temperature.

LEBANESE HOLIDAY

Easter was especially important in our household since it was the only holiday Mom hosted every year. She was the only one of her siblings who had left Michigan, and since everyone else was still in the Detroit area, they had a better argument for why our one household should travel to them on major holidays than we did for why all the rest of them should travel to us. So it was a huge celebration and a significant event in our house. Between all her brothers and sisters, cousins, friends, and neighbors, we hosted between thirty and fifty people every year. And Mom doesn't do buffets, so it was sit-down. Family style, sure, and at several tables, but definitely not a buffet. This is how I learned to host a dinner party. Well, a weekend party, really, since with almost everyone staying overnight it was like camp, with kids sleeping on every available part of the floor (under tables was not unusual). So Easter was a big deal because of the large crowd, but also because of the food we served and the time, energy, and travel it took to secure all the ingredients and prepare everything for the feast. For the raw kibbeh nayeh alone it was no easy feat in rural Ohio every year to find a source for high-quality raw lamb and get it home safely, so this was definitely a special-occasion dish. For the stuffed squash called koosa, we had to make sure we had saved enough of the squash and tomatoes canned the previous summer since the garden would not have produced any yet. And then there were the desserts! While the rest of the year we'd end a meal with fruit—salad made with home-canned fruit in the winter and simple fresh fruit in the summer—Lebanese holidays were another matter altogether. There were trays of homemade baklawa and walnut-filled sambousek, all prepared in advance for Easter Sunday.

Above: Eating with Aunt Jan and Mom

TAWLE MENU

Kibbeh Nayeh
(Ground Raw Lamb with Bulgur), 196

♦

Hummus, Three Ways, 51

♦

Mom's Baba Ghanoush
(Lebanese Eggplant Dip), 56

♦

Stuffed Grape Leaves, 101

♦

Koosa (Stuffed Summer Squash
with Lamb and Rice), 102

♦

Patata Salata
(Lebanese Potato Salad), 80

Sitti's Syrian Rice, 144

♦

Green Beans with Cinnamon
Tomato Sauce, 108

♦

Sfeeha (Meat Pies), 136

♦

Fatayer bi Sabanekh (Spinach Pies), 135

♦

Fruit Plate
with Orange Blossom Syrup, 249

♦

Baklawa, 260

♦

Sambousek (Walnut-Filled
Half-Moon Cookies), 254

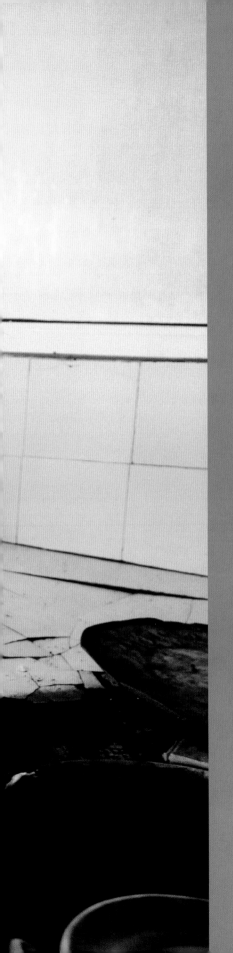

4

Carbs, Beautiful Carbs

Breads, Grains, and Legumes

When I was growing up, we used bread as a utensil at the dining table. Until I traveled in this part of the world, I never knew how common this practice is in Lebanon and elsewhere in the region. We thought it was just a funny quirk of my mom's that Dad enjoyed teasing her about. Today, at the center of every table at Maydān is our Toné Flatbread (page 123), which we make to order in our clay oven. There are always forks and knives available, but we really love when everyone eats with their hands. When bread is at the center of your table it brings the meal together, and the meal brings people together.

The bread was a hot topic when we first opened, because the bread is not rice. People come to a place like ours, where we serve kebabs and all manner of grilled things, and expect to be served rice. We cook primarily on and in a wood-fired grill and clay oven, and these don't lend themselves to cooking up big pots of anything. But I do certainly love rice and other grains and legumes and really carbohydrates in any form, and I'm happy to share a number of those not-bread recipes in this chapter as well. I must admit, though, that nothing would make me happier than for you to try using flatbread as a fork in your house.

Left: A bakery in Lebanon

IN THIS CHAPTER

Top left: Baking lavash in Lebanon

Top right: Making sfeeha at a road side stand, Lebanon

Left: My beloved man'ouche in Lebanon

Toné Flatbread

Makes 18 (6-inch / 15-cm)
round flatbreads

We knew from the beginning of Maydān that the bread was going to be very important to every meal, just as it is in all of the culinary cultures that inspired our menu. Our bread is an amalgamation of several kinds of flatbread we tasted and baked throughout the region, in Lebanon, in Turkey, and in Georgia, where women bake and sell bread along the sides of some roads. In one village in Georgia near the Black Sea, there was a bread oven in front of every hut and seemingly a woman at every oven, baking cinnamon-raisin loaves, the local specialty, and literally waving the loaves at cars as they passed.

Just as the word and concept of the maydān is used in the many languages and countries in the region, so too does similar yet distinct flatbread exist in all of these places. In fact nothing else on our menu expresses our point of view about this region as fully as the bread does. It is both practical and symbolic, and it is the culmination of everything I love about this part of the world. We call it toné, which is what Georgians call the cylindrical stone oven they use to cook their flatbread (photo on page 125), an oven that is incidentally reminiscent of the tandoors used to bake the flat roti in India. We, too, have a wood-fired cylindrical oven, and this is the bread we bake within its walls and serve with every meal at Maydān. Happily, you can make a very good rendition of this bread with a heated pizza stone in a regular oven. And I encourage you to do as we do and urge diners to use it as their utensil, to make each bite unique by pulling and dipping novel combinations of meat, vegetable, herbs, and sauce from all the different dishes on the table.

[recipe continues]

1 tablespoon active dry yeast

1½ tablespoons honey

3 cups (720 ml) warm water (about 110°F / 45°C)

1½ tablespoons canola oil, plus more for the bowl

6 cups (810 g) bread flour, plus more for the work surface

2½ cups (315 g) whole-wheat flour

2 tablespoons kosher salt

In the bowl of an electric stand mixer fitted with the bread hook, whisk together the yeast, honey, and warm water. Let stand until foamy, about 5 minutes. Stir in the oil.

In a separate large bowl, whisk together the bread flour, whole-wheat flour, and salt. Turn the mixer on to low speed and gradually add the flour mixture to the yeast mixture, until all the flour is incorporated, about 8 minutes.

Increase the speed to medium-low and mix until the dough forms a ball and pulls away from the sides of the bowl, 5 to 7 minutes.

Turn the dough out onto a lightly floured work surface. Knead a few times, about 30 seconds.

Form the dough into a ball. Lightly oil a large bowl and transfer the dough to the bowl, turning it over once or twice so it is coated in oil. Cover with a kitchen towel and let stand in a warm place until doubled in size, about 1 hour.

Place a pizza stone on the bottom rack of the oven and preheat the oven to 500°F (260°C).

Lightly dust a work surface with flour. Punch down the dough and cut it in half. Cut each half into 9 pieces (you'll have 18 pieces total) and roll each piece into a ball. Cover the balls with a towel and let stand 10 minutes.

Lightly dust a work surface with flour. Working with one ball at a time, roll each one out into a 6-inch (15 cm) round that is about ¼ inch (6 mm) thick. Arrange the rounds on a floured work surface or floured baking sheets. Cover loosely with plastic wrap and let rise until puffy, about 25 minutes.

Using a lightly floured pizza peel or rimless baking sheet, slide 3 rounds at a time onto the hot pizza stone and bake until the rounds have puffed up and the bottoms are lightly browned, 4 to 5 minutes.

Serve immediately or wrap in aluminum foil to keep warm. Toné is best the day it is made, but it can be reheated with pretty good results.

Wrap leftover bread tightly in aluminum foil and store at room temperature up to 2 days or freeze up to 1 month (defrost at room temperature). Reheat for 5 to 8 minutes in a preheated 300°F (175°C) oven.

Right: Teaching us how to bake using a toné oven

Compass Rose's Khachapuri

Georgian Cheese Bread

Makes 3 (14- to 16-inch / 35.5- to 40.5-cm) cheese breads; 12 servings

For me, the experience of Moscow will forever be intertwined with falling in love with the republic of Georgia. Georgians are so welcoming, and their food and wine go hand in hand with their hospitality. The food of Georgia is very popular in Moscow and the appreciation Muscovites have for the inexpensive, comforting dishes served in Georgian restaurants reminds me of how people in many parts of the United States feel about our neighborhood Mexican places.

In Moscow, I was first introduced to khachapuri, but I had many more opportunities to become acquainted with it on my frequent trips to Georgia. Every region of the country seems to have its own iteration of this delectable stuffed bread, and there's relatively little crossover between regions. This was just fine with me as I love them all, whether they are filled or topped with beans or potatoes or cheese. If I had to pick a favorite, though, it would be one I had in the port city of Batumi in the Adjara region of the country on the Black Sea. Adjaruli khachapuri is boat-shaped, and its "hull" is filled with cheese before baking. As soon as the bread boat comes out of the oven, the baker tops the melted cheese with butter and egg yolk, then vigorously stirs the mixture with two forks until it emulsifies into a liquid lava cheese pool. To eat this masterpiece, diners tear off pieces of bread from the side of the boat and dip them into the pool of cheese (or you can simply slice it and eat it).

If I'm honest, I can't be completely sure that it wasn't the memory of a piping hot, melty, cheesy adjaruli khachapuri that really prompted the birth of my ambitions to open a restaurant. That's right: I opened a whole damn restaurant just to share the glory of khachapuri with the people of DC. But first I had to figure out how to replicate or at least approximate it here. I'll never forget being at the Georgian embassy in Washington, DC, and explaining to the ambassador there our plans to bring khachapuri to the city. The large man studied me for a minute, then he leaned far back in his chair and declared in a deep, accented voice, "You have problem." I waited with bated breath, my mind racing through the mountain of problems I'd already had securing every kind of permit to open my restaurant and trying to imagine what sort of problems I hadn't already faced or at least considered. At last, the man continued, "Cheese is problem." Ah. Challenge accepted. After mountains of research and many thousands of khachapuris, we came up with a mix of cheeses readily available in the U.S. to replace the Sulguni used in Georgia. This combination has just the right saltiness, and its texture is closest to what you get on the streets of Batumi. There must be forty different versions of khachapuri in Georgia, but we make only this one. We do, however, make a lot of it, serving an average of twelve thousand of these beloved "bread boats" every year.

[recipe continues]

For the dough:

1 tablespoon active dry yeast

1 teaspoon sugar

1 cup lukewarm water (about 110°F / 45°C)

3 cups (375 g) all-purpose flour, plus more for the work surface

1 teaspoon kosher salt

Extra-virgin olive oil, preferably Lebanese unfiltered, for the bowl

For the filling:

7 ounces (200 g) mozzarella, grated by hand

6 ounces (170 g) feta cheese, crumbled

5 ounces (140 g) ricotta cheese

For each khachapuri:

1 large egg, beaten

1 large egg yolk

1 tablespoon unsalted butter

Za'atar, preferably Z&Z brand (optional)

To make the dough, in a small bowl, combine the yeast, sugar, and lukewarm water. Let stand until foamy, about 5 minutes.

In the bowl of an electric stand mixer fitted with the bread hook, combine the flour and salt. Add the yeast mixture to the flour and mix on low speed until the dough begins to ball up.

Turn the dough out onto a lightly floured work surface. Knead a few times, about 30 seconds, using as little extra flour as possible.

Form the dough into a ball. Lightly oil a large bowl and transfer the dough to the bowl, turning it over once or twice so it is coated in oil. (The dough may be prepared to this point and placed in the refrigerator overnight or up to 1 day; when ready to proceed, continue as directed.) Cover the dough with plastic wrap and let stand in a warm place until doubled in size, about 1 hour.

Lightly dust a work surface with flour. Cut the dough into 3 equal pieces. Roll each piece into a ball. Cover the balls with plastic wrap and let stand in a warm place for 1 hour.

Meanwhile, to make the filling, in a large bowl, fold together the mozzarella, feta, and ricotta. Divide the filling into 3 equal portions. The filling can be made in advance and stored in a covered container in the refrigerator for up to 1 day or in the freezer for up to 1 month.

Place a pizza stone on the bottom rack of the oven and preheat the oven to 475°F (245°C).

Lightly dust a work surface with flour. Working with one ball at a time, roll it to an oval shape with the longer side running horizontally. Use your hands to gently pull the dough at 9 and 3 o'clock and also at 12 and 6 o'clock into an oblong shape that is 14 to 16 inches (35.5 cm to 40.5 cm) long (at 9 and 3 o'clock) with a wider center that is 6 inches (15 cm) across (at 12 and 6 o'clock).

Fold the end at 9 o'clock over itself and pinch it so it stays sealed. Repeat with the end at 3 o'clock. Generously brush the beaten egg all along the edge of the dough and both folded ends.

Break and scatter one cheese portion in the center of the dough; don't worry about making it perfect—it'll melt and spread in the oven. Repeat with the remaining dough balls and cheese.

Using a lightly floured pizza peel or rimless baking sheet, slide one khachapuri at a time onto the hot pizza stone and bake until the edges are golden brown, 5 to 6 minutes.

Place the khachapuri on a plate, place the egg yolk, butter, and za'atar, if using, on top, and use two forks to stir and fold them into the melted cheese. Continue stirring and folding until the cheese is uniformly mixed; it should look a little like a pool of melted cheese inside a canoe of bread. Serve hot, and invite diners to rip (the bread), dip (the bread into the cheese), and enjoy!

Kartopiliani

Georgian Cheese-and-Potato-Filled Bread

Makes 2 (10-inch / 25-cm) stuffed breads; serves 8

For the dough:

¼ cup (60 ml) milk, heated to lukewarm (about 110°F / 45°C)

2 tablespoons sugar

1 tablespoon active dry yeast

1 cup (240 ml) labne

1 large egg, lightly beaten

2 tablespoons unsalted butter, melted and cooled, plus more for before and after baking

3½ to 4 cups (440 to 500 g) all-purpose flour, plus more for the work surface

1 teaspoon kosher salt

Extra-virgin olive oil, preferably Lebanese unfiltered, for the bowl

For the filling:

1½ pounds (680 g) all-purpose potatoes, peeled and cut into 2-inch (5 cm) pieces

Kosher salt

½ cup (1 stick / 115 g) unsalted butter

2 large onions, chopped

1 teaspoon freshly ground black pepper

I was at an open-air market in Tbilisi the first time I ever tasted warm bread stuffed with potatoes. A woman carrying a bag of them handed one to me in exchange for some Georgian lari. How she kept them all so hot in there, I will never know. And I will also never forget it. Please don't shy away from making this just because it's made of buttery potatoes and bread. Once in a while it's good for the soul to go all in on deliciousness in just this way.

To make the dough, in the bowl of an electric stand mixer fitted with the bread hook (don't attach the bowl to the mixer yet), combine the warm milk and sugar and stir to dissolve the sugar. Sprinkle the yeast on top and let stand until foamy, 5 to 10 minutes.

Heat the labne for 30 seconds in the microwave and stir it into the milk. Stir in the egg and butter until well combined.

Place the bowl on the mixer and add 2 cups (250 g) flour and the salt. Mix on medium-low speed until the flour is thoroughly incorporated, scraping down the sides of the bowl as needed.

Add 1 cup (125 g) flour and continue to mix until thoroughly incorporated, scraping down the sides of the bowl as needed. With the mixer going, add the remaining flour ¼ cup (30 g) at a time, until the dough comes together fully; you may not need all of the flour.

Increase the speed to medium and beat 5 to 10 minutes, until the dough is tacky but does not stick to your hand or the kneading attachment.

Form the dough into a ball. Lightly oil a large bowl and transfer the dough to the bowl, turning it over once or twice so it is coated in oil. Cover the dough with plastic wrap and let stand in a warm place until doubled in size, about 1 hour.

To make the filling, place the potatoes in a large saucepan. Add cold water to cover by 1 inch (2.5 cm) and a couple generous pinches of salt. Bring to a boil over medium-high heat. Reduce the heat and simmer until tender, 12 to 15 minutes.

Drain the potatoes, then use a potato ricer to rice them into a large bowl.

Meanwhile, in a large skillet melt the butter over medium heat. Add the onion and a pinch of salt and pepper and cook until soft and lightly caramelized, about 20 minutes.

Add the cooked onion to the bowl with the mashed potatoes. Add the pepper and salt to taste. Fold to combine; don't overwork the filling. Let cool to warm room temperature.

Place a pizza stone on the bottom rack of the oven and preheat the oven to 400°F (205°C).

[recipe continues]

On a lightly floured work surface, divide the dough in half and form each piece into a ball. Keep one ball covered while you work with the other one.

Roll one ball of dough out to a 12-inch (30.5 cm) circle. Place half of the potato filling in the center, spreading it out in an even layer, leaving a border of about 3 inches (7.5 cm) around the outer edge.

Bring the edges together and pinch them to seal the dough completely, trying not to allow any air to stay trapped inside the package. Sprinkle the sealed side with flour and flip the dough over. Lightly push the round out to about 10 inches (25 cm). Set it on a sheet of parchment or a lightly floured surface, cover with plastic wrap or a kitchen towel, and let rise 30 to 45 minutes.

Repeat with the remaining dough and potato filling to make another stuffed bread.

Brush the tops of the breads with some melted butter. Using a lightly floured pizza peel or rimless baking sheet, slide the breads one at a time onto the hot pizza stone and bake until the tops are browned and the bottoms are lightly browned, about 15 minutes.

Brush the tops of the hot breads with melted butter. Serve hot.

Tightly wrap leftovers in aluminum foil and store at room temperature for up to 2 days.

Talame with Za'atar

Za'atar Bread

Makes 10 (8-inch / 20-cm) rounds

For the dough:

2 cups (480 ml) lukewarm water (about 110°F / 45°C)

¾ teaspoon active dry yeast

Pinch sugar

4 teaspoons vegetable oil, plus more for the bowl

6 cups (750 g) all-purpose flour

3 tablespoons white corn meal

1 teaspoon kosher salt

For the topping:

1½ cups (210 g) za'atar, preferably Z&Z brand

¼ cup (40 g) white sesame seeds

Extra-virgin olive oil, preferably Lebanese unfiltered

There was a bakery in Toledo we'd go to regularly to stock up on pita and other flatbread to bring back home to Ada. They had these delightful round breads topped with za'atar that we call talame. We warm them up and eat them as is for breakfast. On my first trip to Lebanon I realized that this bread is called man'ouche by most of the rest of the world, and it is often rolled with Syrian cheese, mint, tomato, and cucumber. These delectable rolled sandwiches are sold at man'ouche stands all over Lebanon, kind of like how hot dogs are sold all over New York City, only better.

In the bowl of an electric stand mixer fitted with the bread hook, combine the water, yeast, and sugar. Let stand until foamy, about 5 minutes. Stir in the oil.

In a separate bowl, whisk together the flour, corn meal, and salt.

Turn the mixer on to low speed and gradually add the flour mixture to the yeast mixture, until all the flour is incorporated. Increase the speed to medium-low and mix until the dough is smooth and pulls away from the sides of the bowl.

Turn the dough out onto a lightly floured work surface. Knead a few times, about 30 seconds.

Form the dough into a ball. Lightly oil a large bowl and transfer the dough to the bowl, turning it over once or twice so it is coated in oil. Cover with a kitchen towel and let stand in a warm place until doubled in size, about 1 hour.

Place a pizza stone on the bottom rack of the oven and preheat the oven to 475°F (245°C).

Lightly dust a work surface with flour. Cut the dough in half. Cut each half into 5 equal pieces (you'll have 10 pieces total) and roll each piece into a ball. Cover the balls with a towel and let stand 30 minutes.

Meanwhile, to make the topping, in a small bowl, stir together the za'atar and sesame seeds. Add enough olive oil to make a thick paste. Set aside.

Lightly dust a work surface with flour. Working with one ball at a time, pat or roll each one out into an 8-inch (20 cm) round. Brush the tops of the rounds lightly with olive oil. Generously spread the za'atar mixture evenly on top of each.

Using a lightly floured pizza peel or rimless baking sheet, slide 3 rounds at a time onto the hot pizza stone and bake until the rounds have puffed up and the bottoms are lightly browned, 5 to 6 minutes. If desired, heat in the broiler just to brown the tops. Serve hot or warm.

Wrap talame tightly in aluminum foil and store at room temperature for 1 day or freeze for up to 1 month. Defrost at room temperature; if desired, warm in a preheated 300°F (150°C) oven.

Fatayer bi Sabanekh

Spinach Pies

Makes about 40 (3-inch / 7.5-cm) pies

Dough for Sfeeha (page 136)

2 pounds (910 g) trimmed fresh spinach, washed and well dried (see Note)

2 teaspoons kosher salt

2 large onions, finely chopped

½ teaspoon freshly ground black pepper

⅛ to ¼ teaspoon ground allspice

¾ cup (180 ml) fresh lemon juice (from about 6 lemons)

½ cup (120 ml) extra-virgin olive oil, preferably Lebanese unfiltered

½ cup (1 stick / 115 g) unsalted butter, melted, plus more for baking sheets if using

These little bites filled with lemony spinach come from one of my family's most beloved church cookbooks. Their great flavor comes from lots of lemon juice and olive oil. Don't skimp on that liquid, but do be sure to drain off any excess in each spoonful before filling the dough. Then, use the leftover liquid as salad dressing, or do what my mom and aunts do, and drink it! For the cheese version of these pies, see page 240.

Make the dough, let it rise, and divide into 4 equal balls as for sfeeha.

Meanwhile, prepare the spinach filling. Chop the spinach and place it in a bowl. Add the salt and use your hands to massage the salt into the spinach. Set aside for 10 minutes.

Squeeze the excess liquid out of the finely chopped onion and place in a bowl. Add the pepper and allspice.

Squeeze the spinach to remove as much liquid as possible. Add the spinach to the bowl. Toss to evenly disperse the spinach, onion, and spices.

Position a rack in the top third of the oven and preheat the oven to 400°F (205°C). Grease two rimmed baking sheets or line them with parchment paper.

On a lightly floured work surface, working with one ball of dough at a time, roll out the dough to about ⅛ inch (3 mm) thick. Use a 4-inch (10 cm) round cutter to cut out rounds; set aside the dough scraps. Repeat with the remaining dough. Combine the scraps, reroll, and cut out more rounds (you'll have about 40 rounds total).

In a bowl, whisk together the lemon juice and olive oil. When ready to assemble the pies, pour the dressing over the spinach and toss to coat.

Spoon about 1 tablespoon filling into the center of each round, leaving a border of about 1 inch (2.5 cm) all around. Make sure not to add too much liquid to each one (let the filling drain a moment over the bowl before filling the pastry).

To shape the fatayer, bring the sides of the dough up in 3 parts, and pinch together the seams from the base to the top center, so that the package forms a triangle, being sure to completely enclose the filling. Repeat with the remaining dough rounds and filling.

Place the pies about 2 inches (5 cm) apart on the prepared baking sheets. Brush the pies with melted butter. Bake one sheet at a time in the top third of the oven until the crust is lightly browned, 20 to 25 minutes.

Transfer the fatayer to cooling racks to cool. Serve warm or at room temperature. Store any leftover fatayer in a tightly covered container in the refrigerator for up to 1 week.

Note: To get 2 pounds (910 g) trimmed and ready-to-go spinach, you may want to start with as much as 2½ to 3 pounds (1.2 to 1.4 kg) of spinach bunches.

Sfeeha
Meat Pies

Makes about 60 (2-inch / 5-cm)
meat pies; 10 to 12 servings

For the dough:

1 package (2¼ teaspoons) active dry yeast

Pinch sugar

3 cups (720 ml) lukewarm water (about
110°F / 45°C)

½ cup (120 ml) vegetable oil or clarified butter
(page 248), plus more for the bowl

8 cups (1 kg) all-purpose flour, plus about
1 cup (125 g) more for kneading and more for
the work surface

1 tablespoon kosher salt

In Lebanon there are many little shops where they only bake and sell sfeeha, including an amazing stall in the souk in the city of Baalbek, where the old Roman ruins are a popular tourist attraction. Theirs are the very best sfeeha I've ever tasted, and I've sampled my fair share, usually pulling them piping hot out of paper boxes while strolling along dusty streets on a summer day. No one buys fewer than a couple of dozen and then you're meant to eat them all day.

Truthfully there are so many different kinds of small hand pies in Lebanon and all of them are so tasty, which made it hard to choose which ones to include here. The filling for these specific little bites is very similar to what we'd use to fill other meat pies, except that sfeeha contain tomato and other meat pies do not. Since my family usually makes a tomato-less filling, I asked my friend Victoria to share the recipe her family in Chicago has traditionally prepared. She graciously obliged, and I hope you'll love it as much as I do. They are a little labor intensive but get quicker to make as you get the hang of it.

To make the dough, in the bowl of an electric stand mixer fitted with the bread hook, combine the yeast, sugar, and ¼ cup (60 ml) of the warm water. Let stand until foamy, about 5 minutes. Stir in the oil and the remaining 2¾ cups (660 ml) water.

In a separate large bowl, whisk together the flour and salt.

Turn the mixer on to low speed and gradually add the flour mixture to the yeast mixture, until all the flour is incorporated and the mixture forms a smooth dough. Scrape down the sides and to the bottom of the bowl from time to time. Continue to run the mixer for a few minutes after that, 10 minutes from start to finish.

Turn the dough out onto a floured work surface; it will be very sticky. Knead for about 1 minute, adding handfuls of flour (you may need up to 1 cup [125 g]) until the dough is smooth and no longer sticky.

Form the dough into a ball. Lightly oil a large bowl and transfer the dough to the bowl, turning it over once or twice so it is coated in oil. Cover the bowl with plastic wrap and let stand in a warm place until doubled in size, about 1 hour.

Lightly dust a work surface with flour. Turn the dough out onto the surface and divide it into 4 equal pieces. Shape each piece into a ball. Cover the balls loosely with plastic wrap and let stand 20 minutes.

For the filling:

1 tablespoon unsalted butter

⅓ cup (45 g) pine nuts

12 ounces (340 g) ground 90/10 lamb or beef

1 large onion, finely chopped

½ cup (90 g) finely chopped seeded plum tomatoes

½ cup (18 g) fresh flat-leaf parsley leaves

3 cloves garlic, finely chopped with salt (see Note)

1¼ teaspoons kosher salt

3 tablespoons tahini (sesame seed paste), preferably Beirut brand, stirred until smooth before measuring

1 teaspoon ground sumac

½ teaspoon ground allspice

½ teaspoon cayenne pepper or crushed red pepper or smoked paprika

¼ teaspoon ground cinnamon

¼ teaspoon freshly ground black pepper

½ cup (1 stick / 115 g) unsalted butter, melted, plus more for baking sheets if using

Meanwhile, to make the filling, in a skillet, melt the butter over medium heat. Add the pine nuts and cook, stirring, until lightly browned and fragrant, about 1 minute. Quickly transfer the nuts and butter to a dish to stop the cooking; set aside to cool.

In a large bowl, combine the lamb, onion, tomatoes, parsley, garlic, remaining salt, tahini, sumac, allspice, cayenne pepper, cinnamon, black pepper, and the reserved pine nuts. Use your hands to combine the ingredients, working the meat as little as possible.

Preheat the oven to 375°F (190°C). Grease two rimmed baking sheets, or line them with parchment paper.

On a lightly floured work surface, working with one ball of dough at a time, roll out the dough to about ⅛ inch (3 mm thick). Use a 3-inch (7.5 cm) round cutter to cut out rounds; set aside the dough scraps. Repeat with the remaining dough. Combine the scraps and reroll and cut out more rounds (you'll have about 60 rounds total). If at any point the dough springs back too much when you roll it, or the cut rounds shrink excessively, cover the dough with plastic wrap or a kitchen towel and let it rest for 10 to 20 minutes.

Spoon about 1 teaspoon filling into the center of each round and gently pat it down so that there is a border of about 1 inch (2.5 mm) all around.

To shape the sfeeha, lift and pinch together the dough on two opposite sides (at 9 and 3 o'clock). Turn the pastry 90 degrees and pinch together the two other opposite sides. You should have a pretty square shape. If the dough is very sticky, dip your fingers in a little flour.

Repeat with the remaining dough rounds and filling.

Place the pies about 2 inches (5 cm) apart on the prepared baking sheets. Brush the pies with melted butter.

Bake one or two sheets at a time until the crust is lightly browned, about 20 minutes, swapping the sheets if necessary during baking to ensure even browning.

Transfer the sfeeha to cooling racks to cool. Serve warm or at room temperature. Store any leftover sfeeha in a tightly covered container in the refrigerator up to 1 week.

Note: Chop the garlic, then sprinkle about ¼ teaspoon of the salt on top, and continue to chop it very fine. When adding it to the other ingredients, scrape it and any juices into the bowl together.

Tita's Meat Pies
Lahme bi Ajeen

Makes about 60 (3-inch / 7.5-cm)
or about 40 (4-inch / 10-cm)
half-moon pies

1½ pounds (680 g) ground lamb

½ cup (1 stick / 115 g) unsalted butter,
cut into pieces

1 medium onion, minced

1 teaspoon kosher salt

1 teaspoon freshly ground black pepper

¼ cup (35 g) pine nuts, toasted (page 55)

4 cups (520 g) Bisquick

2 cups (250 g) all-purpose flour

2 cups (480 ml) milk

½ cup (1 stick / 115 g) unsalted butter,
melted, plus more as needed and for
baking sheets, if using

The two previous pies are delicious, but it takes a bit of time to make the dough and fillings, enough time that it puts them squarely in the category of special-occasion food for my family. This is likely why many years ago Tita (that's what we called my great-grandmother) came up with these very tasty shortcut pies. Quickly cooking the lamb eliminates the need to fuss with a raw meat filling, and a Bisquick dough considerably shortens the time from bowl to oven to plate. Don't fret if there is leftover filling; it makes a great topping for hummus (page 51).

Brown the lamb in a frying pan until no longer juicy. Add the butter, onion, salt, pepper, and pine nuts. Cook until the onions are soft, about 8 minutes. Remove from the heat and let cool to room temperature.

Preheat the oven to 425°F (220°C). Butter two rimmed baking sheets or line them with parchment paper.

In a large bowl, stir together the Bisquick and flour. While stirring, add the milk gradually. Mix and knead the dough until combined and soft. Divide the dough in half.

On a lightly floured work surface, working with one piece of dough at a time, roll the dough ⅛ inch (3 mm) thick.

Use a round 3- to 4-inch (7.5 to 10 cm) cutter to cut out rounds; reroll the scraps if necessary. Repeat with the remaining dough (you'll have about 60 smaller or 40 larger rounds).

Spoon about 1 tablespoon filling into the center of each round; use a little less than 1 tablespoon for the smaller rounds and a little more for the larger rounds. Fold the top half down to cover the filling and the bottom half, forming a half-moon shape. Gently press to seal the edges together. Repeat with the remaining dough rounds and filling.

Place the pies ½ inch (12 mm) apart on the prepared baking sheets. Brush each pie with melted butter. Bake until lightly browned on both the top and the bottom, 12 to 15 minutes.

Serve warm or at room temperature. Store leftovers in an airtight container in the refrigerator up to 3 days or in the freezer up to 1 month. Defrost at room temperature and reheat and recrisp in a preheated 300°F (150°C) oven.

Maqluba
Upside-Down Rice with Eggplant

Serves 6

In September 2019, David and I were invited to visit Karam House in Reyhanli, Turkey, a tiny town on the border with Syria. The house is run by the Karam Foundation, an organization based in Chicago whose primary mission is to care for Syrian refugee youth in Turkey and Jordan. Their objective at Karam House is manifold and critical: to meet the educational, social, and emotional needs of the children and young people who have been displaced from their homeland because of the brutal, protracted civil war there. For one incredible week we taught the kids a few American dishes and learned some delicious Syrian dishes and so very much more from them. I can't imagine a more moving and instructive experience than we had there with those resilient kids. Plus we prepared the most amazing food together. It included this showstopper, layered rice and meat and eggplant that is turned out onto a platter and topped with a crown of buttered, toasted nuts. The trick is to get it out of the pan perfectly, a task so daunting to the students that many of them had to call their moms (also safely in Turkey) for guidance. I would never make light of any of what these kids have lived through, and yet somehow their simple act of calling their moms for cooking advice was as poignant and touching as anything else I heard or learned that week. By the way, please don't be afraid to try this! The key to success is a good, nonstick pot; you can find inexpensive and reliable ones online.

Karam is run by founder and CEO Lina Sergie Attar, who very kindly shared recipes for many of the dishes we made together, including this one, which was featured in a cookbook Karam themselves put together several years ago to highlight many of the incredible women they have helped over the years. This recipe originally came from a woman named Um Haythem, who was born in Syria in 1910 and became a certified obstetric nurse and the mother of six children, as well as being well known among her friends and family for her Ramadan specialties.

[recipe continues]

1 medium eggplant (about 1 pound / 455 g), stem trimmed, sliced lengthwise ⅜ inch (1 cm) thick

½ cup (120 ml) extra-virgin olive oil, preferably Lebanese unfiltered, plus more as needed

Kosher salt

1 pound (455 g) stew beef (chuck or round), cut into 1½-inch (4 cm) cubes

2 large onions, 1 quartered and 1 finely chopped

1½ teaspoons Baharat (page 149)

3 cups (720 ml) boiling water

8 ounces (225 g) ground beef

3 cups (570 g) Egyptian rice or other medium-grain rice, such as Arborio

5 tablespoons (70 g) unsalted butter

¼ cup (30 g) cashews

¼ cup (30 g) slivered almonds

¼ cup (35 g) pine nuts

Equipment: 6-quart (5.7 liter) nonstick pot

Preheat the oven to 425°F (220°C).

Place the eggplant slices in a single layer on a baking sheet and brush each side with olive oil, using about ¼ cup (60 ml) total, and season very lightly with salt. Bake until nicely browned on the bottom, 15 to 20 minutes. Flip the slices over and continue baking until browned on the other side, 5 to 10 minutes. Set aside until needed.

Meanwhile, in a medium saucepan, heat 2 tablespoons of the olive oil over medium-high heat until shimmering. Add the cubed beef with the quartered onion, ¾ teaspoon Baharat, and 1 teaspoon salt; stir to coat all the ingredients with oil. Increase the heat to high and cook until the meat is browned, stirring frequently, about 10 minutes.

Add the boiling water, cover the pan, reduce the heat, and simmer until tender, about 1 hour. Strain, reserving meat and broth separately; discard the onion.

In a sauté pan, heat the remaining 2 tablespoons olive oil over medium heat until shimmering. Add the chopped onion and cook, stirring often, until softened and translucent, 6 to 8 minutes. Add the ground beef with the remaining ¾ teaspoon Baharat and 1 teaspoon salt and cook, breaking up the meat, until browned, about 5 minutes. Set aside.

To assemble the maqluba for cooking, in a 6-quart nonstick pot, evenly spread the ground beef across the bottom. Evenly scatter the beef cubes on top. Arrange the eggplant slices on top of the beef so that the narrow ends overlap across the center of the pan and the rounded ends run 2 to 3 inches (5 to 7.5 cm) up the side of the pan. When all the slices are arranged, they'll make a sort of flower or star pattern.

Evenly scatter the rice on top, using it to keep the eggplant slices in place. Try to make sure that very little rice finds its way between the parts of the eggplant that are against the pan and the pan sides. This will ensure that you can see the eggplant when the maqluba is turned out.

Measure the reserved broth and add enough water to bring the total to 4½ cups (1 liter). Gently pour the broth over the rice (again, do this slowly so that the rice doesn't move too much). Add 3 tablespoons (40 g) of the butter. The liquid should go about 1 inch (2.5 cm) over the top layer; add more water if necessary.

Cover the pot and cook over medium-low heat until the rice is cooked and all the liquid is absorbed, 30 to 35 minutes. Set aside, covered, for 10 minutes then uncover.

Meanwhile, melt the remaining 2 tablespoons butter in a cast-iron or other heavy skillet over medium heat. Add the cashews and cook, stirring, until just beginning to brown, about 6 minutes. Add the almonds and cook, stirring, until the almonds are just beginning to brown, 2 to 3 minutes. Add the pine nuts and cook, stirring until all the nuts are golden brown, about 1 minute. Remove the nuts from the pan. Set aside.

Place a large round serving dish over the uncovered pot. Carefully flip over the pot so the meat is now on the top and the eggplant slices are visible around the perimeter. Sprinkle with the browned nuts and serve warm.

Tahdig
Persian Rice with Crisp Crust

Serves 10 to 12

4 cups (720 g) long-grain basmati rice

3 tablespoons kosher salt

Vegetable oil

¼ cup (60 ml) labne or plain full-fat yogurt

¼ teaspoon crumbled saffron plus 1 tablespoon warm water (optional; see Note)

1 tablespoon unsalted butter

Pomegranate seeds, for garnish (optional)

Equipment: 6-quart (5.7 liter) nonstick pot

After so many of our Persian guests talked to us proudly about this beloved rice dish with a beautiful crispy top, we actually figured out how to cook it on the fire at Maydān, but it's sufficiently challenging that we only do it for special events.

For home cooking, my dear Persian friend Sameen, who lives in Los Angeles, gave me her recipe. There are various ways to achieve the delectable crisp crust that is the hallmark of this dish, and this method, which uses oil and labne in the crust and employs a towel wrapped around the lid to trap steam inside (a specially made damkesh can be used instead), is one of the more authentic ones, which is part of why I was especially eager for her recipe. I can't stress enough that a straight-sided 6-quart (5.7 liter) pan is truly necessary for best results.

Put the rice in a bowl and rinse until the water runs clear. Drain well.

Fill a 6-quart (5.7 liter) nonstick pot with water. Add the salt and bring to a boil.

Add the drained rice to the boiling water with 2 tablespoons oil. Cook until the rice is nearly fully cooked but still has a slight chew, about 10 minutes. Drain the rice and rinse with cold water to stop the cooking.

Rinse and dry the pot. Pour in ¾ cup (180 ml) oil and add the labne. Whisk to combine and evenly disperse the labne; it's fine if it looks separated.

Add a little more than 2 cups (350 g) of the cooked rice to the pot and pat it down to form a flat layer at the bottom of the pot. Add the remaining rice in an even layer on top.

Cut the butter into several pieces and scatter them on top of the rice. Cover the pot and cook over high heat for 4 minutes.

Reduce the heat to medium-low. Wrap a kitchen towel around the outer rim of the pot and lid to cover the gap between them and catch the escaping steam. Cook for 30 minutes.

Remove the pot from the heat and carefully unwrap it (the towel will be hot, so be careful). Uncover the pot. Run a thin butter knife or offset spatula around the outer edge of the rice. Place a large serving plate upside-down over the pot. Holding both the plate and the handles of the pot, quickly flip them in a single motion to unmold the tahdig onto the plate. If any of the crispy topping remains in the pan, simply scrape it out and top the rice with it, and tell everyone that it's exactly as you intended it to be. Garnish with pomegranate seeds, if using. Serve hot or warm.

Note: If you'd like to add saffron to the crisp topping, dissolve it in the warm water. Add to the oil and labne and whisk together.

Sitti's Syrian Rice

Serves 6 to 8

3 tablespoons unsalted butter

1 pound (455 g) coarsely ground lamb (optional)

1 stalk celery, finely chopped

¼ cup (35 g) pine nuts, toasted (see page 55)

2 cups (370 g) white rice, preferably Ben's Original, or a medium-grain rice such as Arborio or Egyptian

4 cups (960 ml) good-quality low-sodium chicken broth

2 teaspoons kosher salt

½ teaspoon ground cinnamon, or to taste

Rice cooked with ground lamb and pine nuts (which you can see on page 109) is what we called simply "rice" in my house, and it was a staple dish that Mom made several nights a week. Note that the lamb in this recipe is certainly optional, and though Mom may not agree, I think it's quite delicious with or without it. While it may come as a surprise to rice purists, my mom and her siblings rely on Ben's Original (which is the much-improved, modern name for what was called "Uncle Ben's" back then). I don't know where the reliance on the brand came from, but it was ubiquitous across generations of my family, as my grandmother and her sisters also kept a healthy supply of the stuff in their pantries. I gained a little insight into this curious habit when we went to my grandfather's village in Lebanon and my cousin's wife insisted that the best choice was what she called "Egyptian rice." I'd heard this before, from friends with close ties to or who had learned to cook in Lebanon. When I finally tracked it down on a subsequent trip to Lebanon, I saw that it resembles and cooks up like Arborio rice, which is to say that it's a quite fluffy, white rice, perfect for using in the many rice dishes my family loves. Perhaps that's the standard that my relatives were trying to emulate and that's what led them to rely on a rice that also yields very fluffy results every time.

In a large saucepan, melt the butter over medium heat. Add the lamb, if using, celery, and pine nuts and cook, stirring occasionally, until the meat is browned. Stir in the rice until it is very well combined with the meat. Add the chicken broth, salt, and cinnamon.

Bring to a boil. Stir once, cover the pan, and lower the temperature to a simmer. Cook until the rice is tender and the broth is absorbed, 15 to 20 minutes; if the liquid is absorbed before the rice is cooked, add a little water.

Let stand, covered, for 10 minutes. Fluff the rice and serve.

Harissa Couscous

Serves 4 to 6

For the sweet harissa:

Kosher salt

1 medium carrot, peeled and sliced ½ inch (12 mm) thick

1 red bell pepper, roasted (see page 35) and coarsely chopped

½ habanero chile or 2 serrano peppers, halved, seeds and ribs removed, and chopped

1 clove garlic, minced

1 tablespoon fresh lemon juice, plus more if needed

1 teaspoon tomato paste

2½ teaspoons coriander seed, toasted (see page 39) and ground

1¼ teaspoons caraway seed, toasted (see page 39) and ground

Pinch ground cloves

Extra-virgin olive oil, preferably Lebanese unfiltered, for storing

For the couscous:

1½ teaspoons extra-virgin olive oil, preferably Lebanese unfiltered

1 strip orange zest, removed with a vegetable peeler

1 clove garlic, crushed with garlic press

1 (3-inch / 7.5-cm) cinnamon stick

1 bay leaf

½ teaspoon kosher salt

1 cup (195 g) couscous

¼ cup (60 ml) hot water, or as needed

¼ cup (13 g) chopped fresh flat-leaf parsley

When we developed the Tunisian Chicken Skewers (page 181) for Compass Rose, we knew we would serve it with a traditional accompaniment of couscous, but we wanted the couscous to be something special on its own, so we folded in some harissa we made. This is not the harissa that we created at Maydān a few years later (page 35), first and foremost because it didn't exist yet; but even if it had, I don't think we'd have used it in this dish. For a couscous to go with the smoky Tunisian chicken, this slightly sweeter and milder harissa fits the bill beautifully. And I'm certainly not breaking conventions by having two different harissa recipes in this book; in Tunisia and Morocco there are infinite variations of the sauce. You can see how we serve this couscous in the photo on page 180.

To prepare the harissa, fill a small saucepan a few inches deep with water and add a generous pinch of salt. Bring to a boil. Add the sliced carrot, reduce the heat, and simmer until tender, about 20 minutes.

Drain the carrot and place it in a food processor. Add the roasted bell pepper, habanero, garlic, lemon juice, tomato paste, coriander, caraway, and cloves. Process until the mixture is almost puréed with a bit of texture; it's okay if it's a little chunky. Taste and adjust the seasoning with salt or lemon juice.

The harissa can be made in advance. To store, transfer it to a container with a tight-fitting lid. Smooth the top and pour over enough olive oil to cover the surface. Cover the container and refrigerate up to 1 month.

To prepare the couscous, in a medium saucepan put the olive oil, orange zest, garlic, cinnamon stick, bay leaf, salt, and 1½ cups (360 ml) water. Bring to a boil over high heat.

Place the couscous in a medium metal bowl. Pour the boiling water and all the aromatics into the bowl with the couscous and stir to combine. Cover the bowl tightly with plastic wrap, being careful because the bowl will be hot. Let stand for 10 minutes. (The plastic wrap might form a dome; once the dome depletes the couscous should be ready.)

Uncover the couscous and fluff it with a fork; remove and discard the orange zest, cinnamon stick, and bay leaf.

In a separate small bowl, carefully whisk together the harissa and ¼ cup (60 ml) hot water. It should be pourable; add water as needed if it is not.

Pour about half of the thinned harissa over the couscous and add the parsley. Stir and toss to combine. Taste and add more harissa if desired, or adjust the seasoning with salt.

Serve hot, warm, or at room temperature.

Mandi

Syrian Charcoal–Flavored Chicken Rice

Serves 4 to 6

For the chicken:

1 roasting chicken (about 4 pounds / 1.8 kg)

2 tablespoons Baharat (page 149)

1½ teaspoons kosher salt

½ teaspoon ground turmeric

2 tablespoons extra-virgin olive oil, preferably Lebanese unfiltered, or more as needed

For the rice:

3 cups (540 g) basmati rice

2 teaspoons Baharat (recipe follows)

2 teaspoons kosher salt

1½ teaspoons ground turmeric

2 bay leaves

For serving:

1 tablespoon grapeseed or other neutral vegetable oil for the bowl

1 tablespoon extra-virgin olive oil, preferably Lebanese unfiltered, or more as needed

¼ cup (25 g) sliced almonds

¼ cup (35 g) raisins

Ezme (optional; page 37)

Equipment: Chunk of charcoal; small metal bowl or aluminum foil for charcoal

When we were learning about Syrian food from the kids at Karam House in southern Turkey (see page 139), there was a moment when a couple of the students came to get me specifically to show me a technique they somehow knew would surprise me. When I reached the stove, I witnessed a truly charming method of smoking food that I'd never seen before. The chicken and rice were cooked and put in the pan together, then a block of charcoal was lit aflame and placed inside a little bowl tucked into the rice. They put the lid in place and left it for several minutes. The result was beautifully smoked and very flavorful chicken and rice. The method is so simple and the results so delicious that I can't believe I'd never seen it before.

To spatchcock the chicken for even roasting, place it breast side down on a cutting board. Starting at the neck end, use poultry shears or a sharp boning knife to cut along one side of the backbone toward the tail, stopping your cut about two-thirds of the way down the length of the backbone. Repeat on the other side of the backbone. Now cut down the last bit of length on either side to completely remove the backbone.

Flip the chicken over and press down hard on center of the breast to make it lie flat. Tuck the wing tips under the wing bone.

In a small bowl, combine the Baharat, salt, turmeric, and oil. Stir into a thick but spreadable paste; add more oil if necessary to achieve this consistency. Rub the paste all over the chicken. Place uncovered in the refrigerator for at least 1 hour and up to 24 hours.

Preheat the oven to 450°F (230°C).

Place the flattened chicken, breast side up, on a rack in a roasting pan. Roast for 15 minutes. Reduce the oven temperature to 350°F (175°C) and roast until the juices run clear when the thickest part of the thigh is pierced with a sharp knife, 35 to 45 minutes. Remove from the oven and let stand for 5 to 10 minutes. Cut the chicken in half down the length of the breastbone. Set aside.

Meanwhile, to cook the rice, rinse the basmati until the water runs clear. Drain well.

Pour 4½ cups (1 liter) water into a large Dutch oven or other heavy pot with a tight-fitting cover and add the Baharat, salt, turmeric, and bay leaves. Bring to a boil. Stir in the rice and return the water to a boil. Cover the pot, reduce the heat, and simmer for 15 minutes, until the water is absorbed and the rice is just tender to the bite. Remove from the heat and let stand, covered, for 5 minutes.

Have ready a small metal bowl or make a small bowl out of several sheets of aluminum foil.

[recipe continues]

Place the charcoal briquette on the gas flame, directly on the electric rings of the stovetop, or in the broiler until bright red and very hot.

Uncover the pot and fluff the rice; remove and discard the bay leaves. Place the two chicken halves side by side on top of the rice. Tuck the small bowl between the chicken halves and nestle it in the rice. Pour about a tablespoon of vegetable oil into the bowl. Use tongs to carefully transfer the hot charcoal into the bowl. Immediately cover the pot and let stand for 10 minutes.

To make the garnish, in a small skillet, heat the olive oil over medium-low heat until shimmering. Add the almonds and cook, stirring, until lightly browned, about 2 minutes. Use a slotted spoon to transfer the almonds to a small dish to cool. Add the raisins to the oil and cook, stirring, for 2 minutes. Add to the plate with the almonds and set aside.

Just before serving, uncover the pot and remove the dish of charcoal. Cut the chicken into pieces, arrange them on top of the rice, and sprinkle with fried raisins and almonds. Serve, passing the ezme in a separate bowl.

Or you can bring the whole pot to the table so that everyone can enjoy the smoky and dramatic uncovering. Cut the chicken into pieces and serve with the smoky rice. Top each serving with fried raisins and almonds. Pass the ezme separately.

Baharat

Makes about 1 cup (95 g)

***

¼ cup (25 g) sweet paprika

¼ cup (25 g) ground cumin

2 tablespoons freshly ground black pepper

2 tablespoons ground coriander

1 tablespoon ground nutmeg

1 tablespoon ground cinnamon

1½ teaspoons ground cardamom

1½ teaspoons ground cloves

***

The word *baharat* means "spices" in Arabic, and it is also the name given to this mixture of warm spices. Variations of the mix are used liberally throughout this part of the world; this is Maydān's version of the blend. For very bold flavor and longer shelf life, grind as many of the spices as possible yourself before mixing them together, but it's also absolutely fine to use pre-ground spices.

In a small bowl, stir together the paprika, cumin, pepper, coriander, nutmeg, cinnamon, cardamom, and cloves. Store in an airtight container in a cool, dark place for up to 6 months.

Itch
Armenian Bulgur Wheat Salad

Serves 6 to 8

1½ cups (210 g) medium bulgur wheat

Kosher salt

3 cups (720 ml) boiling water

¼ cup (60 ml) red pepper paste (see Note)

6 tablespoons pomegranate molasses, plus more for serving

¼ cup (60 ml) extra-virgin olive oil, preferably Lebanese unfiltered

2 tablespoons tomato paste

2 tablespoons fresh lemon juice (from about 1 lemon)

1 tablespoon Aleppo pepper flakes

2 cups (300 g) sliced shishito peppers

1 cup (110 g) sliced green onions, white and green parts

½ cup chopped tomato, for serving (optional)

I first had this hearty and very flavorful dish on our first research trip for Maydān. Earthy bulgur is brightened by pomegranate molasses and crunchy shishitos and green onions. One bite and I knew the dish was coming home with us.

Place the bulgur and ½ teaspoon salt in a medium bowl. Pour over the boiling water, cover the bowl with plastic wrap, and set aside until the bulgur is tender but still chewy and the water is absorbed, about 25 to 30 minutes.

Drain the bulgur using a fine-mesh strainer and then squeeze it to release as much of the water as possible. Use a fork to fluff the bulgur and spread it on a rimmed baking sheet to cool completely.

In a separate bowl, whisk together the red pepper paste, pomegranate molasses, olive oil, tomato paste, lemon juice, Aleppo pepper flakes, and ½ teaspoon salt.

Place the cooled bulgur into a large bowl and toss with the dressing, shishito peppers, and most of the green onions (set some aside for garnish). Taste and season with salt if necessary. Transfer to a serving dish. Drizzle over some pomegranate molasses and garnish with the remaining green onions and tomatoes, if using. Serve.

Note: Use a mild red pepper paste, not chili paste or Indonesian sambal oelek or Korean gochujang (although both of those taste amazing). If you can't find mild red pepper paste, drain a small jar of piquillo or other mild red peppers and puree them.

Dango

Omani Garlic–Butter Chickpeas

Serves 6 to 8

6 tablespoons (85 g) unsalted butter

5 cloves garlic, finely chopped

¾ teaspoon Aleppo pepper flakes

⅛ teaspoon sweet paprika

4 cups (750 g) barely cooked, drained chickpeas (page 52; see Note)

⅓ cup (75 ml) fresh lime juice (from 4 to 6 limes), plus more as needed

1½ tablespoons kosher salt, plus more as needed

½ teaspoon freshly ground black pepper

Extra-virgin olive oil, preferably Lebanese unfiltered, for serving

Ground sumac, for serving

We always have this very simple Omani dish on the winter menu at Maydān because it's warming and full of comforting flavors, like butter and garlic and a little kick of chile. It's very similar to a Lebanese dish called *balila*, but I prefer dango because everything tastes better with butter. Since the star of the show here is the chickpeas, I urge you to follow the super simple method on page 53 for cooking your own from dried. The butter gives the dango's brothy sauce a beautiful, velvety texture.

In a large saucepan, melt the butter over medium heat. Add the garlic and sauté until softened and very fragrant, about 1 minute. Add the Aleppo pepper and paprika and cook until fragrant, about 30 seconds.

Stir in the chickpeas, lime juice, salt, pepper, and 3 cups (720 ml) water. Bring to a gentle boil, then reduce the heat and simmer, uncovered, until the liquid is reduced by about half and the chickpeas are very tender, about 1 hour.

Taste and add more lime juice or salt as needed. Transfer to a serving dish. Drizzle over some olive oil and sprinkle with sumac. Serve hot.

Note: Follow the directions on page 52 to cook the chickpeas until just barely done. They'll continue to cook as you prepare them here.

Imjaddarah

Lentils and Rice with Crispy Onions

Serves 6 to 8

3 large onions

6 tablespoons (90 ml) extra-virgin olive oil, preferably Lebanese unfiltered

1 cup (190 g) brown lentils, rinsed and picked through

1 cup (185 g) long-grain white rice

1½ teaspoons kosher salt

1 teaspoon freshly ground black pepper

This dish demonstrates beautifully how humble ingredients often hold the greatest, most rewarding surprises. Lentils and rice are perfectly fine and very common partners. It's when you top them with a generous pile of fried onions that their union comes close to pure bliss.

Dice one of the onions and thinly slice the other two onions. Set aside separately.

In a large saucepan, heat 2 tablespoons of the oil over medium heat. Add the diced onion and cook, stirring, until translucent, about 5 minutes.

Add the lentils, rice, 1 teaspoon salt, ½ teaspoon pepper, and 3½ cups (840 ml) water to the pan and bring to a boil. Cover the pan, reduce the heat, and simmer until the rice and lentils are cooked, about 30 minutes.

Remove the pan from the heat and let stand, covered, for up to 10 minutes.

Meanwhile, heat the remaining 4 tablespoons (60 ml) oil in a sauté pan over medium heat. Add the sliced onion and remaining ½ teaspoon salt and ½ teaspoon pepper and cook, stirring occasionally, until golden brown, 15 to 20 minutes.

To serve, stir the lentils and rice thoroughly and pour onto a serving platter. Top with the sautéed onions and any oil in the pan. Serve warm.

Kushari

Egyptian Elbow Pasta with Lentils, Chickpeas, and Rice

Serves 6 to 8

For the fried onions:

Canola oil, for deep-frying

1 large onion

⅔ cup (80 g) all-purpose flour

Kosher salt

For the tomato sauce:

1½ tablespoons extra-virgin olive oil, preferably Lebanese unfiltered

1 pound (455 g) plum tomatoes, diced

½ cup (55 g) diced onion

1½ tablespoons tomato paste

4 cloves garlic, finely chopped

1½ tablespoons cumin seed, ground

1 teaspoon kosher salt

½ teaspoon freshly ground black pepper

2½ tablespoons distilled white vinegar

For the rice:

2 tablespoons unsalted butter

1¾ ounces (50 g) thin vermicelli or crushed angel hair pasta (about ¼ cup)

½ cup (95 g) brown lentils, rinsed and picked through

1 cup (220 g) short-grain white rice

2½ teaspoons cumin seed, ground

2 teaspoons kosher salt

½ teaspoon freshly ground black pepper

For the pasta:

8 ounces (225 g) uncooked elbow pasta

Kosher salt

Extra-virgin olive oil, preferably Lebanese unfiltered

For the chickpeas:

1½ cups (175 g) cooked, drained chickpeas (page 52) or 1 can (15 ounces / 425 g) chickpeas, with their cooking or canned liquid

Kosher salt

Kushari is a traditional and very delicious Egyptian street food. For years a longtime bartender at Compass Rose named Mo, who is originally from Egypt, exhorted us to add it to the menu. He talked so longingly about this fantastic plate of carbs layered one on top of the other that soon enough we did indeed add it. But no matter how hard we pushed it, Americans just weren't going for it. Perhaps its ingredients don't hint enough at all the flavor and texture that the full dish delivers. I don't know the reason, but we did eventually pull it from the menu. I've never given up on kushari, though, and I don't regret a thing. It is at its absolute best when you deep-fry the onion for the dish yourself, but if that step is enough to dissuade you from trying it, please don't let it! Simply pan-fry some onion as for Imjaddarah (page 154) or use store-bought fried onions instead.

To prepare the fried onions, in a deep heavy pot such as a Dutch oven, pour canola oil to a depth of 3 inches (7.5 cm); make sure that the surface of the oil is at least 3 inches (7.5 cm) below the top rim of the pan. Heat the oil to 300°F (150°C) according to a deep-fry thermometer over medium heat, about 30 minutes. Line a baking sheet or platter with paper towels and place next to the stovetop.

While the oil is heating, peel the onion, cut it in half, and slice it as thinly as possible. Toss the sliced onions in the flour and shake to remove the excess flour.

Carefully drop a couple of handfuls of onions in the oil. Don't crowd the pan; do this in batches. Cook until deeply browned, 3 to 4 minutes, carefully flipping over the onions with a spider or slotted spoon once or twice so that they cook evenly.

Using the spider or slotted spoon, transfer the onions to the paper towels. Season with a few pinches of salt. Continue with the remaining onions and set aside.

To prepare the tomato sauce, heat the olive oil in a large sauté pan over medium heat until it shimmers. Add the tomatoes and diced onion and cook until the onion is softened and the tomato has cooked down, about 15 minutes.

Stir in the tomato paste, garlic, cumin, salt, and pepper and cook over medium heat for 10 minutes. Add 2 cups water (480 ml) and bring to a low simmer. Simmer for 15 minutes. Stir in the vinegar and return to a simmer. As soon as the sauce comes to a simmer, turn the heat off.

Use an immersion blender to blend the tomato mixture until smooth. Set aside and keep warm.

[recipe continues]

To prepare the rice, melt the butter in a medium saucepan over medium heat. Add the vermicelli and cook, stirring, until golden brown, about 5 minutes. Add the lentils and 2 cups (480 ml) water and bring to a gentle boil. Reduce the heat and simmer for 10 minutes.

Add the rice, cumin, salt, pepper, and 1 cup (240 ml) water. Increase the heat to medium-high and bring to a simmer. Reduce the heat, cover the pan, and simmer until the rice and lentils are tender and the liquid is completely absorbed, about 25 minutes. Uncover and let stand for 5 minutes. Fluff with a fork.

To prepare the pasta, bring a medium saucepan of salted water to a boil. Add the pasta and cook until al dente, about 11 minutes, or as directed on the package. Drain well, drizzle over some olive oil, and toss to coat. Set aside.

Meanwhile, gently warm the chickpeas in their liquid. Add salt to taste. Drain them and set them aside, kept warm.

To serve, spread the fluffed rice mixture on a serving platter. Top with the pasta and about half of the tomato sauce, then the chickpeas, and finally finish with about half of the fried onions. Serve, passing the remaining tomato sauce and fried onions separately.

Lahmajoun
Armenian Lamb Pizza

Makes 4 (10-inch / 25-cm) pizzas

For the crust:
½ recipe of the dough for Toné Flatbread (page 123), prepared through the first rise

For the topping:
1 large onion, chopped

¼ cup (35 g) chopped roasted red pepper (page 35 or use drained store-bought)

2 tablespoons tomato paste

1¾ teaspoons ground allspice

1¼ teaspoons Aleppo pepper flakes

1¼ teaspoons kosher salt

1 pound (455 g) very cold ground lamb

⅓ cup (45 g) pine nuts (optional)

All-purpose flour, for rolling out the dough

Extra-virgin olive oil, preferably Lebanese unfiltered

Pomegranate molasses, for serving (optional)

This highly seasoned minced or ground lamb spread on flatbread (which you can see on page 160) makes a great snack or quick lunch and it's always a welcome addition to a big feast. Lahmajoun is honestly delicious in any setting, and especially so at a very cool Armenian-owned shop called Ichkhanian that's been operating in Beirut forever. Their lahmajoun, which you can order drizzled with pomegranate molasses if desired, is among the best in the city. That's the main reason I love the place, but I would be remiss if I didn't mention that part of what makes it so fascinating is its location. During the Lebanese Civil War from 1975 to 1990, the Green Line, which was a line of demarcation that separated the predominantly Muslim part of Beirut from the predominantly Christian part of the city, ran directly in front of the building that houses Ichkhanian. And the building has the bullet holes to prove it.

Divide the rested dough into 4 equal balls. Cover the balls with a towel and let stand 10 minutes.

Place a pizza stone on the bottom rack of the oven and preheat the oven to 500°F (260°C).

To prepare the topping, place the onion, red pepper, tomato paste, allspice, Aleppo pepper flakes, and salt in a food processor and process just until chopped and well blended. Add the lamb and pulse a few times just to blend the ingredients lightly.

Transfer the mixture to a large mixing bowl. Add the pine nuts, if using, and use a spatula to combine the mixture evenly (do this even if you don't add the pine nuts). Divide the mixture into 4 equal portions—leave them in the bowl if desired—and refrigerate until needed.

Lightly dust a work surface with flour. Working with one ball at a time, roll out each ball into a 10-inch (25 cm) round and set aside, loosely covered with plastic wrap, while you roll the others.

Transfer one rolled-out round to a piece of parchment or a lightly floured baking peel or rimless baking sheet (this will make it easier to transfer it to the oven). Brush it lightly with olive oil and use a silicone or rubber spatula to spread one portion of the lamb mixture on top, spreading right to the edge of the dough.

Slide the pizza onto the hot pizza stone and bake until the edges are lightly browned, 4 to 5 minutes. Continue with the remaining dough balls, brushing each one with olive oil before topping with a portion of lamb.

Just before serving, drizzle over some pomegranate molasses, if using. Serve.

Euphrates
Maydān's Favorite No-Booze Cocktail

Serves 1

Ice, for mixing and serving

3 ounces (90 ml) gin alternative

1½ ounces (45 ml) Mint Simple Syrup (see recipe at right)

1½ ounces (45 ml) fresh lime juice

Fresh mint leaf and fresh mint sprig, for garnish

Lime wheel, for garnish

Equipment: Highball glass and cocktail pick

Our guests come from all over the world as well as our neighborhood, and many of them don't drink alcohol for all sorts of reasons. But it's not just teetotalers who are responsible for the popularity of this drink. The Euphrates is almost as popular with people who love a good boozy cocktail as it is with everyone else.

Fill a cocktail shaker with ice. Add the gin alternative, syrup, and lime juice. Shake vigorously to chill the drink.

Fill a highball glass with ice. Strain the drink into the glass. Skewer the mint leaf and lime wheel on a cocktail pick. Garnish with the pick and fresh mint sprig. Serve.

Mint Simple Syrup

Makes 16 ounces (480 ml)

***

2 cups (400 g) sugar

2 cups (100 g) fresh mint leaves

***

In a medium saucepan combine the sugar, mint leaves, and 2 cups (480 ml) water.

Bring to a gentle boil over medium-high heat, stirring with a wooden spoon until the sugar is dissolved.

Cover the pan and remove it from the heat. Let stand 15 minutes.

Strain and discard the mint leaves. Let cool.

Transfer to a jar and store in the refrigerator up to 2 weeks.

GEORGIAN SUPRA

Among the best things about our time in Moscow was learning more about the delightful people of Georgia, for whom hospitality and generosity are second nature, especially their tradition of supra, an hours-long dinner led by a tamada, or toastmaster. On our first trip there, our charming local guide, Dato, invited David and me to a supra at one of his favorite restaurants. When we arrived, our hostess led us straight out the back and through the door of one of several little wooden huts outside the main restaurant built specifically for supras. Dato cheerfully described the evening to come, that he would be our tamada for the evening, leading each of twelve toasts throughout the meal, and how the kitchen would send out a feast of dishes as they were ready. Pork skewers called mtsvadi; khinkali, piping hot meat dumplings; platters of fresh herbs and pickled vegetables, including jonjoli, the super sour pickled flowers that are a staple of the Georgian pantry; plus the eggplant rolls, badrijani nigvzit, and chicken in creamy satsivi sauce, two of the incredible walnut dishes I'd first enjoyed early in our stint in Moscow (page 12); and then different variations of khachapuri. The food didn't stop coming for more than two hours; dishes only cleared when every morsel was gone from them, new plates simply balanced on top of those already set unless something needed refreshing, like when the remaining now-cold khinkali were whisked back to the kitchen, where they were browned in hot butter and returned to us, now crisped and warm. And every few minutes, Dato would refill our glasses with wine or the strong Georgian brandy called *chacha* and deliver another toast—to God, to Georgia, to children, to the deceased, to David and me, and on and on until I lost count, wrapped in the warmth of the cozy little hut and the people in it, full of food and wine and chacha and happiness. I had fallen in love with this country and its people and the tradition of hospitality that is woven into the fabric of their whole lives. And floating above it all was the delightful aroma of blue fenugreek, which since then has been, to me, the scent of Georgia.

TAWLE MENU

Badrijani Nigvzit (Georgian Eggplant
Rolls with Walnut Filling), 88

◆

Khinkali (Georgian Meat-Filled
Dumplings), 204

◆

Chicken Satsivi
(Chicken in Walnut Sauce), 213

◆

Gebjalia (Georgian Cheese Rolls
with Mint), 235

Lobio Mtsvanilit (Georgian Herbed
Kidney Beans), 106

◆

Compass Rose's Khachapuri
(Georgian Cheese Bread), 126

◆

Kartopiliani (Georgian Cheese-and-
Potato-Filled Bread), 129

◆

Adjika (Georgian
red pepper sauce)

5

Food on a Stick

Kebabs

Compass Rose was founded on the culinary theme of street food, which is often presented on a stick. Countless times over the years, David and I have gotten lost in big cities and small towns alike, and no matter where we are, we almost always find delicious and cheap food threaded onto a stick . . . kebab shops in Lebanon, mishkak in Oman, or almost anywhere in Turkey, where the entire restaurant culture is based on kebabs. I've even developed a hypothesis about kebabs in the places I've been in this part of the world. I am convinced that they are the gateway to each country's flavor palate, and that if you stop at a kebab stand on the side of the road just inside the border of any country in this area, the spices used to season what you're eating will be what you taste throughout your visit there. Though I haven't been able to test this hypothesis in a scientifically rigorous way, I continue to collect data by eating as many kebabs as I can wherever I go, including right here in the U.S. It's fascinating how even in countries where there is a big wealth disparity, the people on the streets eating kebabs come from every part of society, no matter their means. Kebabs are a kind of equalizer both within and between these different countries and cultures. And in my experience, they're also a really approachable way to introduce people to new spices and flavors. One important thing that not everyone knows, though, is that flatbread is the ideal tool for pulling the components off the skewers and daubing them in sauces to make each of your individual bites, or bakoun, as my mom would say (see page 29).

Left: Chef Darnell at the hearth at Maydān

IN THIS CHAPTER

Right: Shawarma maker, Oman

Bottom: Mishkak stand, Muscat, Oman

Far right: Cooking with grandmas, Oman

Top to bottom: Lahme Mishwe (opposite) and Aleppo Lamb Kebabs (page 173)

Lahme Mishwe
"Grilled Meat" Lamb Kebabs

Serves 6 to 8

2 pounds (910 g) lean lamb, cut into
1½- to 2-inch (4 to 5 cm) cubes (see Note)

Yogurt Saffron Marinade or Whiskey (or Not)
Marinade (recipes follow; optional)

Kosher salt and freshly ground black pepper

3 sweet onions, cut into thick wedges

1 pint (340 g) cherry tomatoes (optional)

3 bell peppers, one each red, yellow, and green,
or any color, cored and cut into 1½-inch (4 cm)
pieces (optional)

8 ounces (225 g) cremini mushrooms, stems
removed, caps halved if large (optional)

Vegetable oil, for the grill

For serving:
Flaky sea salt (such as Maldon)

Ezme (page 37)

Toum (page 34)

Flatbread

Equipment: 4 to 6 skewers; if bamboo or wood,
soak them in water for 30 minutes before using.

Summertime during my childhood included many evenings eating lamb kebabs that had been grilled in our backyard. Always joined on the skewers by wedges of onion and occasionally by red and green bell pepper as well, the chunks of lamb were seasoned only with salt and pepper. I still adore simply seasoned lamb, but when we put lamb kebabs on the menu at Maydān, naturally the chefs wanted to add a little something more. Chefs do *love* marinades, and here are two favorites from the kitchen, a tangy saffron-and-yogurt affair and a deep, cumin-y one that Chef Darnell Thomas brought back with him from Lebanon. He learned it with whiskey, from my chef friend Bethany (see page 236) but since so many of our guests follow a halal diet, which does not include alcohol, we were happy to learn that it is just as good without the booze.

If using the marinade, put the lamb chunks in a nonreactive bowl or zip-top plastic bag and pour over the marinade. If using a bowl, toss to coat and cover the bowl with plastic wrap. If using the bag, seal it and massage the outside of the bag to make sure the meat is well coated in marinade. Refrigerate for at least 1 hour and up to overnight.

If not using the marinade, generously season the lamb cubes with salt and pepper.

Prepare a hot grill.

Thread the lamb and onions on the skewers, as well as the cherry tomatoes, bell peppers, and mushrooms, if using. Season the threaded kebabs with salt and pepper.

Lightly grease the grill grate with oil and add the skewers. Grill, rotating the kebabs every few minutes, until the meat and vegetables are browned in parts, 10 to 12 minutes for medium-rare.

Transfer the cooked kebabs from the grill directly to a platter and sprinkle with flaky salt. Serve, passing bowls of ezme and toum and the flatbread separately.

[recipe continues]

Yogurt-Saffron Marinade

Makes about 2 cups (480 ml)

***

¼ teaspoon crushed saffron threads

1 tablespoon rose water

½ cup (120 ml) labne

½ cup (120 ml) extra-virgin olive oil, preferably Lebanese unfiltered

2 tablespoons fresh lime juice (from about 1½ limes)

1½ teaspoons honey

½ yellow onion, thinly sliced lengthwise

6 cloves garlic, crushed with a garlic press

Grated zest of 1 orange

1 teaspoon kosher salt

½ teaspoon freshly ground black pepper

¼ teaspoon ground turmeric

***

In a small dish, combine the saffron and rose water. Let stand at least 5 minutes to dissolve the saffron.

In a medium bowl, place the labne, olive oil, lime juice, honey, onion, garlic, orange zest, salt, pepper, and turmeric. Add the saffron and rose water, and stir to combine.

Use or store in an airtight container in the refrigerator for up to 4 days.

Whiskey (or Not) Marinade

Makes about 2 cups (480 ml)

***

½ cup (120 ml) labne

⅓ cup (75 ml) extra-virgin olive oil, preferably Lebanese unfiltered

¼ cup (60 ml) whiskey or water

1 white onion, chopped

½ bunch green onions, white and green parts, thinly sliced

4 cloves garlic, chopped

2 tablespoons fresh lemon juice (from about 1 lemon)

1 tablespoon ground cumin

½ tablespoon freshly ground black pepper

½ tablespoon sweet paprika

¾ teaspoon Aleppo pepper flakes

***

In a blender, place the labne, oil, whiskey, white onion, green onion, garlic, lemon juice, cumin, black pepper, paprika, and Aleppo pepper flakes. Blend until the ingredients are chopped and well combined.

Use or store in an airtight container in the refrigerator for up to 4 days.

Syrian Seven Spice

Makes about ¾ cup (70 g)

Lebanon and Syria may be very close geographic neighbors, but when it comes to using spice, the distance between them is significantly wider. This blend of seven spices is a great example; it is uniquely Syrian. The region in Lebanon my grandmother is from is very close to Syria. They have and use all of the spices in this mix, but they don't combine them this way, which is why I had never seen these familiar spices blended until I traveled to the region and tasted Syrian food.

***

¼ cup (30 g) freshly ground black pepper

¼ cup (30 g) smoked Spanish paprika, preferably La Chinata sweet

2 tablespoons ground coriander

1 tablespoon ground cloves

2 teaspoons ground nutmeg

2 teaspoons ground cinnamon

1 teaspoon ground cardamom

***

In a small bowl, stir together the pepper, paprika, coriander, cloves, nutmeg, cinnamon, and cardamom. Store in an airtight container in a cool, dark place for up to 6 months.

Aleppo Lamb Kebabs

Grilled Minced Lamb Kebabs

Serves 6 to 8

6 tablespoons minced garlic

3 tablespoons extra-virgin olive oil, preferably Lebanese unfiltered, plus more for the grill

2½ teaspoons Syrian Seven Spice (recipe on previous page)

2 pounds (910 g) very cold ground lamb

2¾ teaspoons kosher salt

½ teaspoon baking soda (see Note)

Vegetable oil, for the grill

Flaky sea salt (such as Maldon), for serving

Sumac Onion and Herb Salad (page 79), for serving

Equipment: 6 to 8 skewers; if bamboo or wood, soak them in water for 30 minutes before using.

In Syria, these kebabs (see the photo on page 170) are extra delicious because they often contain fat from the tail of Awassi sheep, which are bred in part for their wonderful backsides. Here in the States, I go to a Lebanese butcher and ask them to grind some lamb shoulder or another cut that is nicely marbled with fat. Mixing the ground meat in a stand mixer for several minutes gives the meat a pleasing springiness when it's grilled. Be sure the meat is very cold when it goes into the mixer.

In a blender combine the garlic, oil, and Syrian Seven Spice and blend until smooth.

Put the lamb in the bowl of an electric stand mixer fitted with the paddle attachment. Add the garlic mixture, salt, and baking soda to the bowl. Mix on medium-low for 2 for 3 minutes, scraping down the sides of the bowl, until the mixture is thoroughly blended and tacky to the touch.

Wet your hands with cold water and divide the meat into 6 to 8 equal portions and mold each around a skewer like a corndog. Transfer the skewers to a baking sheet or platter. Cover and refrigerate until ready to grill (up to 4 hours).

Prepare a hot grill.

Lightly grease the grill grate with vegetable oil and add the skewers. Grill, rotating the kebabs every few minutes, until evenly browned and slightly charred in parts, 5 to 10 minutes.

Sprinkle with flaky salt and serve with the Sumac Onion and Herb Salad.

Note: Adding baking soda to the ground meat for kebabs helps to bind together the ground meat and keep the mixture light.

Beef Koobideh
Persian Minced Beef Kebabs

Serves 6 to 8

¼ teaspoon crushed saffron threads

1 tablespoon boiling water

1½ yellow onions, cut into wedges

3 cloves garlic, chopped

2 pounds (910 g) very cold 80/20 ground beef

2¾ teaspoons kosher salt

2¼ teaspoons freshly ground black pepper

¼ teaspoon baking soda

Vegetable oil, for the grill

Flaky sea salt (such as Maldon), for serving

Sumac Onion and Herb Salad (page 79), for serving

Equipment: 8 to 10 skewers; if bamboo or wood, soak them in water for 30 minutes before using.

People who like saffron love these kebabs, and with good reason, as the saffron really shines through beautifully. As with the Aleppo Lamb Kebabs (page 173), be sure the ground beef is very cold before it goes into the mixer.

In a small dish, combine the saffron and boiling water. Set aside.

Process the onion and garlic in a food processor until very finely chopped. Transfer to a sieve and drain for 20 minutes. Press out any excess liquid.

Put the ground beef in the bowl of an electric stand mixer fitted with the paddle attachment. Add the onion and garlic. Mix on low for 1 minute to mix thoroughly. Add the reserved saffron-infused water, salt, pepper, and baking soda. Mix on low until well combined, about 2 minutes.

Scrape down the sides of the mixer. Increase mixer speed to medium-low and mix for 9 minutes, until the mixture is thoroughly mixed and tacky to the touch.

Wet your hands with cold water, divide the meat into 8 to 10 equal portions, and mold each around a skewer like a corndog. Transfer the skewers to a baking sheet or platter. Cover and refrigerate until ready to grill (up to 4 hours).

Prepare a hot grill.

Lightly grease the grill grate with oil and add the skewers. Grill, rotating the kebabs every few minutes, until evenly browned and slightly charred in parts, 5 to 10 minutes.

Sprinkle with flaky salt and serve with the Sumac Onion and Herb Salad.

Omani Beef Tenderloin Kebabs

Serves 4 to 6

For the Omani spice mix:

3½ teaspoons cumin seed, ground

3½ teaspoons fennel seed, ground

1 tablespoon ground ginger

1 tablespoon Aleppo pepper flakes

2¾ teaspoons ground cinnamon

2½ teaspoons ground nutmeg (see Note)

2½ teaspoons coriander seed, ground

2½ teaspoons pink peppercorns, ground

2¼ teaspoons ground turmeric

2 teaspoons black peppercorns, ground

2 teaspoons ground cardamom

2 teaspoons ground dried black lime
(see page 183)

1½ teaspoons whole cloves, ground

5 whole star anise, ground

For the Omani marinade:

¼ cup (24 g) Omani spice mix from above

6 tablespoons grapeseed oil

2 tablespoons extra-virgin olive oil, preferably
Lebanese unfiltered

4 cloves garlic, crushed with a garlic press

2½ pounds (1.2 kg) beef tenderloin, cut into
2-inch (5 cm) pieces

2 tablespoons Omani spice mix from above

Kosher salt

Extra-virgin olive oil, preferably Lebanese
unfiltered, plus more for the grill

Flaky sea salt (such as Maldon), for serving

**Equipment: 4 to 6 skewers; if bamboo or wood,
soak them in water for 30 minutes before using**

When we returned from Oman with a package of a delightful spice mix we'd had there, we asked a local spice merchant to help us recreate the blend. He did so beautifully, using whole spices so we could grind it as needed at Maydān. Here, I've brought the quantities down and converted a few of them to the ground versions that are more likely to be in your spice cabinet. This is a long list of individual spices, but combining them creates a warm and tangy blend to rub on any kind of meat before grilling.

To make the spice mix, in a small bowl, combine the ground spices: cumin, fennel, ginger, Aleppo pepper, cinnamon, nutmeg, coriander, pink peppercorn, turmeric, black peppercorn, cardamom, dried black lime, cloves, and star anise. Stir together until very well blended. This makes a scant 1 cup (90 g). Store in a dark place in an airtight container up to 6 months.

To make the marinade, in a small bowl, combine the Omani spice mix with the grapeseed oil, olive oil, and garlic. Stir until well blended. Put the beef pieces in a bowl or zip-top plastic bag and pour the marinade over them. Stir or rub the bag to coat all of the pieces in marinade. Refrigerate 1 hour or up to 24 hours.

When ready to cook, remove the meat from the refrigerator and thread on skewers. Pat the meat dry and sprinkle with 2 tablespoons Omani spice mix and generously season with salt.

Prepare a hot grill.

Lightly grease the grill grate with oil and add the skewers. Grill, rotating the kebabs every few minutes, until the meat is browned in parts, 8 to 10 minutes for medium-rare.

Transfer the cooked kebabs to a platter, sprinkle with flaky salt, and serve.

Note: If your nutmeg is whole, cut a kernel in pieces and grind it in a spice grinder. Do not grate the nutmeg because grated nutmeg is much lighter than ground, so you'd need much more of it than what's called for here.

Spiced Beef Tenderloin Kebabs: For a quicker and also very tasty version of these kebabs, replace the marinade with double the spice blend from Ribeye with Georgian Dry Rub (page 206) or ¼ cup (24 g) ras el hanout. Rub the beef all over with the spices and put the pieces in a covered bowl or zip-top bag. Refrigerate 1 hour or up to 24 hours. When ready to cook, thread on skewers as instructed and generously season with salt. Continue as directed above.

Kebab bel Karaz

Cherry Kebabs

Serves 6

For the meatballs:

2 pounds (910 g) 80/20 ground lamb or beef

2 tablespoons pine nuts, toasted (page 55) and finely chopped

1 teaspoon Syrian Seven Spice (page 173)

2 teaspoons kosher salt

½ teaspoon freshly ground black pepper

For the cherry sauce:

3 pounds (1.4 kg) fresh or frozen sour cherries, thawed if necessary and pitted; or 2 pounds (910 g) sour cherries and 1 jar (16 ounces / 454 g) sour cherry jam

½ cup (100 g) sugar (unless using the sour cherry jam), plus more to taste

Fresh lemon juice, plus more to taste (optional)

2 tablespoons unsalted butter

1 teaspoon ground cinnamon, plus more for serving

1 teaspoon kosher salt

For serving:

2 to 3 pitas, cut into triangles

2 tablespoons pine nuts, toasted (see page 55)

½ cup (25 g) chopped fresh flat-leaf parsley

Many people use the word *kebab* to mean food that is cooked on a skewer, but in this region the term is used for any grilled meat, whether it's whole or ground and formed into a patty or sausage. The inimitable Lina Sergie Attar, founder and CEO of the Karam Foundation (page 139), shared her family's cherry kebab recipe so I could include it in this collection. It comes from her mom, Safa, who learned it from her own mother, and this is especially lucky for us because Lina has told me that families often prefer to keep the spices they use in their cherry kebabs a closely guarded secret. This specialty of Aleppo relies on dark sour cherries that grow in northern Syria for their unique sweet-and-sour flavor. Here in the U.S., the sour, or tart, cherry season is a fairly short period in June and July. Thankfully they freeze very well, so I recommend buying in season and freezing them to make this dish any time of year. Don't use regular sweet cherries for this dish, for they are far too sweet and the sauce will be cloying. The sauce should be tangy and tart; if the sour cherries are on the sweeter side, add a bit of lemon juice to balance it out.

Preheat the oven to 350°F (175°C).

Put the lamb in the bowl of an electric stand mixer fitted with the paddle attachment. Add the pine nuts, Syrian Seven Spice, salt, and pepper to the bowl. Mix on medium-low for 2 to 3 minutes, until the mixture is thoroughly blended and tacky to the touch.

Scoop up small amounts of the lamb mixture and roll into 1-inch (2.5 cm) balls; wet your hands with water if the mixture is sticking to them. Arrange them without crowding on a rimmed baking sheet.

Bake the meatballs until cooked through, about 10 minutes. Set aside.

Meanwhile, process 2 pounds (910 g) cherries in a food processor until finely chopped. Transfer them to a large Dutch oven or other heavy pot.

Add the remaining 1 pound (455 g) whole cherries or the jar of jam, if using, and ½ cup (100 g) sugar, if using. Bring to a gentle simmer over medium-high heat, reduce the heat to medium, and simmer until the syrup is thickened and silky, 45 to 50 minutes. Taste and add lemon juice or more sugar to adjust the tang-to-sweet ratio.

Add the butter, cinnamon, and salt along with the cooked meatballs. Simmer until the meat is well coated in the sauce and the flavors are melded, 10 to 15 minutes.

To serve, place the pita triangles on a large platter. Arrange the meatballs on top and drizzle with any cherry sauce still in the pot. Garnish with the pine nuts, parsley, and a pinch of cinnamon.

Armenian Pork Skewers

Serves 4 to 6

2½ pounds (1.2 kg) pork butt or shoulder (the fattier the better), cut into 1½- to 2-inch (4 to 5 cm) pieces

1 white onion, thinly sliced, plus 1 white onion, thinly sliced just before serving

1 tablespoon kosher salt

1 tablespoon sweet paprika

1 tablespoon dried summer savory

Vegetable oil, for the grill

Thin lavash, for serving

Leaves from 1 bunch fresh flat-leaf parsley, chopped, for serving

Flaky sea salt (such as Maldon), for serving

Equipment: 4 to 6 skewers; if bamboo or wood, soak them in water for 30 minutes before using

To drive from Tbilisi, Georgia, to Yerevan, Armenia, you must take the twistiest, turniest, most terribly scary mountain road I've ever been on. I can't believe anyone is allowed to drive it. There is one truly redeeming feature on this death trap, though: the man at the kebab stand located on the side of the road midway between the two cities. He cooks pork kebabs, which are simply seasoned and lip-smackingly good. I've had them both on and off that road, and I can attest that it's not purely the joy of being alive that makes them so unforgettable. To recreate them, I turned to my dear friend from graduate school Bella, who grew up in Armenia. Use well marbled pork; lean pork isn't nearly as good here.

Place the pork in a bowl with half of the thinly sliced onions. Season with the salt, paprika, and summer savory. Use your hands to mix the ingredients together until the pork is thoroughly coated in seasoning and the onion is evenly dispersed. Cover and refrigerate 2 to 3 hours.

When ready to cook, thread the pork on skewers.

Prepare a hot two-zone fire in a charcoal grill with a lid: Light a hot fire. When the coals are covered with gray ash, rake them to one side of the grill, creating a cooler zone on the other side to use for indirect cooking. Lightly grease the top grate with oil and put it in place.

Place the skewers over direct heat and grill the pork, turning often, to lightly brown on all sides, 1 to 2 minutes per side.

Transfer the skewers to the ambient heat side (away from the direct heat). Cover the grill, arranging the lid so that the vent is directly over the skewers; open the vent. Cook until tender, 10 to 15 minutes.

Spread the lavash on a platter or in a serving bowl and put the cooked pork on top. Scatter with the freshly cut onion and parsley, sprinkle with flaky salt, and serve.

Tunisian Chicken Skewers on a bed
of Harissa Couscous (page 145)

Tunisian Chicken Skewers

Serves 4

2 tablespoons extra-virgin olive oil, preferably Lebanese unfiltered

½ small onion, thinly sliced

1 red bell pepper, seeded and chopped

½ cup (120 ml) drained mild Peppadew peppers, plus ¼ cup (60 ml) brine from the jar

½ cup (75 g) raisins

¼ cup (60 ml) pomegranate molasses

¼ cup (40 g) roasted unsalted peanuts

¼ teaspoon cayenne pepper

Kosher salt and freshly ground black pepper

1½ pounds (680 g) skinless, boneless chicken thighs, cut into 1½-inch (4 cm) pieces

Harissa Couscous, for serving (optional, page 145)

Equipment: 4 to 6 skewers; if bamboo or wood, soak them in water for 30 minutes before using.

These have been on the Compass Rose menu almost without a break since the very first day we opened in 2014. The few times we've pulled them, our guests definitely noticed, and none more than my husband. It's one of his favorite dishes and not only because the tender, spiced chicken is delicious; David is the reason these particular skewers are on the menu in the first place. During the Arab Spring he and his NPR producer waited in Tunisia for several weeks for the Libyan government to let them enter the country to cover the uprisings there. By the time they were finally granted visas, David had fallen hard for these chicken skewers, an affection that only deepened during their dreary and often nerve-wracking stay in Tripoli, where he ate so badly that he lost almost twenty pounds.

After making the marinade mixture, be sure to hold some of it back as directed to use as a dipping sauce for the grilled skewers.

In a medium nonstick skillet, heat the olive oil over medium-low heat. Add the onion and cook, stirring occasionally, until lightly caramelized, about 20 minutes.

Transfer the onion and oil to a blender. Add the bell pepper, Peppadew peppers and brine, raisins, pomegranate molasses, peanuts, and cayenne to the blender. Purée until smooth. Add 1 teaspoon salt and ½ teaspoon black pepper and pulse once or twice to combine. Set aside about 1 cup (240 ml) for serving with the chicken.

Place the chicken in a medium bowl. Pour over the remaining marinade and rub the marinade into the pieces of chicken. Cover and refrigerate for at least 30 minutes and up to 3 hours.

Light a medium-high grill. Thread the chicken onto the skewers (discard the marinade) and season with salt and pepper.

Grill the skewers, turning often, until lightly charred and cooked through, 10 to 12 minutes.

Pour the reserved dipping sauce into four small dishes. Serve the skewers with the dipping sauce and Harissa Couscous, if using.

Omani Shrimp Kebabs

Serves 6 to 8

1 quart (960 ml) grapeseed or canola oil

6 whole dried arbol or guajillo chiles, stems removed

7 dried black limes

10 cloves garlic, chopped

3 tablespoons tamarind paste or concentrate

3 pounds (1.4 kg) peeled, tail-on (16/20) shrimp

Flaky sea salt (such as Maldon), for serving

Lime wedges, for serving

Equipment: 10 to 12 skewers; if bamboo or wood, soak them in water for 30 minutes before using.

We visited Oman during one summer, and it was so hot that practically nothing happened during the day. When the sun finally went down, we were delighted to find that many little mishkak stands that sell kebabs were open then. In Muscat, Oman, we were told that the best food was in fact in an area by the airport known for its street stalls. There we saw vendor after vendor with the same thing: kofta (ground meat) and regular kebabs. What stuck out above all the other tastes were the shrimp kebabs we got at one stand—they had a kind of fire to them.

We were determined to get the recipe from the very confused proprietor, who gamely entertained our many questions while we scribbled down notes in the dark, but mostly he couldn't fathom why we cared so much. Between our notes and what we managed to communicate between us using only the common language of food, we figured out that their marinade included tamarind, lime, and local chiles. A bit of trial and error upon our return to DC led to this recipe for the best grilled shrimp I've ever had. I love using dried black limes, which add a zesty sourness to dishes and drinks. These limes are dried whole, and many of them turn black during the process, though don't be alarmed if you see much paler ones. They can be found whole and ground in Lebanese, Persian, and Indian grocery stores and online. Before grinding whole limes yourself, break them up first by crushing them under a heavy pot.

In a blender combine the oil, chiles, dried black limes, and garlic. Blend until the ingredients are very well broken down, so that there are no big chunks of lime or garlic. Add the tamarind paste and pulse until well combined. Set aside ½ cup (120 ml) of the marinade.

Place the shrimp in a large bowl and pour the remaining marinade over them. Stir gently so that all of the shrimp are coated in marinade. Cover and marinate in the refrigerator for at least 30 minutes and no more than 3 hours.

Prepare a medium-high grill.

Thread the shrimp on the skewers, being careful not to push them too close together. Grill for 1 to 2 minutes per side, until the shrimp are opaque and pink. Remove them from the grill and brush them with the remaining marinade.

Sprinkle with flaky salt and serve with lime wedges.

Persian Swordfish Kebabs

Serves 6

For the marinade:

1 cup (240 ml) grapeseed or other neutral vegetable oil, plus more as needed

½ cup (120 ml) extra-virgin olive oil, preferably Lebanese unfiltered

¼ cup (60 ml) fresh orange juice (from about 1 orange)

2 cups (80 g) chopped fresh cilantro

1 onion, peeled and quartered

4 cloves garlic, peeled

2 serrano peppers, chopped

2 tablespoons coriander seed, ground

2 tablespoons ground dried black lime (see page 183)

2¼ teaspoons ground turmeric

½ teaspoon black peppercorns, ground

2 pounds (910 g) swordfish, cut into 2-inch (5 cm) pieces

For the finishing glaze:

½ cup (120 ml) fresh orange juice (from about 2 oranges)

½ cup (20 g) chopped fresh cilantro

½ cup (1 stick / 115 g) unsalted butter, cut in pieces

Vegetable oil, for the grill

Flaky sea salt (such as Maldon), for serving

Equipment: 4 to 6 skewers; if bamboo or wood, soak them in water for 30 minutes before using.

As a native-born Midwesterner I really empathize with people who don't enthusiastically enjoy eating all kinds of fish. I'm sure it's different today, but when I was a kid in the eighties fresh fish just wasn't a thing we had. These citrusy fish kebabs are a delicious way to enjoy fish off the grill and help the fish-averse to love it; at the restaurant we also do these kebabs with salmon or monkfish, depending on what's available.

To make the marinade, in a food processor, place the oils, orange juice, cilantro, onion, garlic, serranos, ground coriander, ground lime, turmeric, and pepper. Process until a grainy paste is achieved, adding more oil as needed to thin the mixture and keep it moving.

Put the swordfish in a bowl and add the paste. Use your hands to rub the paste all over the pieces of swordfish. Cover the bowl and refrigerate for at least 30 minutes and up to 2 hours.

Meanwhile, to make the finishing glaze, combine the orange juice and cilantro in a small saucepan. Bring to a simmer over medium heat and cook until the orange juice is reduced by half. Stir in the butter until melted. Set aside.

Prepare a medium-hot grill. Thread the swordfish on the skewers.

Lightly grease the grill grate with oil and add the skewers. Grill, rotating the kebabs every few minutes, until the fish is browned in parts, 8 to 10 minutes.

Transfer the cooked kebabs from the grill directly to a platter. Brush with the finishing glaze and sprinkle flaky salt on the kebabs. Serve.

Shish Taouk
Chicken Kebabs

Serves 4

For the marinade:

¾ cup (180 ml) Toum (page 34)

2 teaspoons fresh lemon juice

1 teaspoon pomegranate molasses

1½ tablespoons cumin seed, toasted (see page 39) and ground

2 teaspoons whole fenugreek seed, toasted (see page 39) and ground

2 pounds (910 g) skinless boneless chicken thighs or breasts, cut into 1½- to 2-inch (4 to 5 cm) pieces

Kosher salt and freshly ground black pepper

For serving:

Sumac Onion and Herb Salad (page 79)

Toum (page 34)

Batata Harra (page 94)

Mouneh (page 62) or store-bought pickles

Salatet Malfouf (page 83)

Equipment: 4 to 6 skewers; if bamboo or wood, soak them in water for 30 minutes before using

With some time to kill before our flight at the very end of one of our trips to Beirut we ended up at a hotel bar, crowded around a platter piled with chicken kebabs and flatbread and toum and potatoes and pickles. It was perched atop a tiny, wobbly table many times smaller than it should have been, and yet, as precarious as the whole setup was, it was very easy to enjoy every delicious bite. The warm feelings that flooded through us as we ate every last morsel on that platter inspired us to make sure we always have shish taouk on the menu at Maydān. I like to think that a fellow traveler who needs to fill a few hours before their flight out of DC might have a similar experience with us one evening. I always make this with boneless chicken thighs, which are in my opinion far tastier (and cheaper!) than boneless chicken breasts, but there is absolutely no reason beyond that for me to insist that you do as I do. Use whatever you have or enjoy the most.

To make the marinade, in a medium bowl combine the toum, lemon juice, pomegranate molasses, cumin, and fenugreek and stir until well blended.

Add the chicken and stir to coat the pieces very well. Marinate in the refrigerator at least 4 hours and up to overnight.

Light a medium-high grill. Thread the chicken onto the skewers (discard the marinade) and season with salt and pepper. Grill the skewers, turning often, until lightly charred and cooked through, 10 to 12 minutes.

Serve the shish taouk with Sumac Onion and Herb Salad on top or alongside and pass the toum, batata harra, mouneh, and salatet malfouf separately.

Dead Sea

Sweet-and-Sour Margarita

Makes 14 (5-ounce / 150-ml) cocktails

For the passion fruit base:
1 pound (455 g) passion fruit purée

6 ounces (180 ml) Simple Syrup (page 112)

2 serrano peppers, chopped

For the drink:
1 (750 ml) bottle joven mezcal

1 (375 ml) bottle blue curaçao

5 ounces (150 ml) Ancho Reyes Verde Liqueur

6 ounces (180 ml) fresh lime juice (from 10 to 12 limes)

For rimming the glasses:
2 tablespoons Aleppo pepper flakes

2 tablespoons urfa biber flakes

2 tablespoons kosher salt

1 lime, cut in half

For serving:
Ice

Dehydrated or fresh orange slices, for garnish

Equipment: Rocks glasses, for serving

The beautiful color of this cocktail brings to mind the gorgeous body of water (not actually a sea, but rather a salt-rich lake) for which it is named. And naturally our Dead Sea isn't merely a pretty sip; its fruity, spicy flavor profile is bold enough that it can stand on its own and food-friendly enough that it's a great partner to almost any dish, and especially with the kebabs in this chapter. We make a big yield here because the whole batch can be mixed and poured out of a pitcher if you're serving a crowd. Or the batch can be kept in the refrigerator for up to one glorious and very tasty month. If you'd prefer to have less on hand, simply cut the recipe in half (or more).

Urfa biber, which makes up part of the salt rim, is a dried chile pepper from Turkey named for the town it comes from. It has a raisiny flavor and color, with deep, not sharp, heat that's a very pleasant component in a cocktail.

To make the passion fruit base, in a medium saucepan, combine the passion fruit purée, simple syrup, and chopped serrano peppers. Heat over medium heat until the mixture reaches a light simmer, then remove from heat. Cover and let stand for 30 minutes. Strain through a fine-mesh sieve and store in a tightly covered container in the refrigerator for up to 1 week.

To make the drink, in a large bowl combine the passion fruit base with the mezcal, curaçao, Ancho Reyes, lime juice, and 1½ cups (360 ml) water and whisk until thoroughly blended. Transfer to bottles or other containers and store in the refrigerator for up to 1 month.

To make the rim salt, in a small bowl combine the Aleppo pepper flakes, urfa biber, and kosher salt. Use a fork to stir thoroughly. Set aside until ready to serve.

To serve, pour the rim salt onto a small plate. Rub the cut side of a lime around the outside of a glass, then lightly turn the rim in the rim salt. Fill the glass with ice. Pour the drink over and garnish with a dehydrated or fresh orange slice.

Left: Drew at the bar

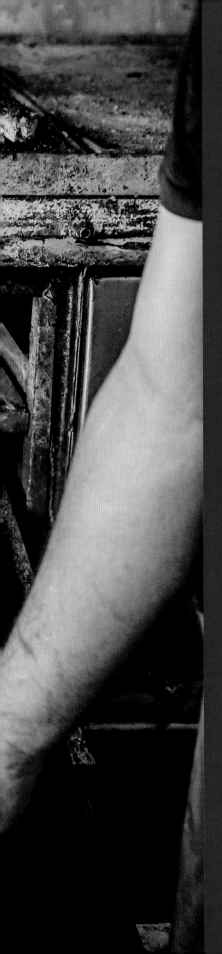

6

You Don't Eat Meat?!

*It's Okay, I Make Lamb
(Meat, Poultry, Fish, and Shellfish)*

Before I write a single word to introduce the recipes on the following pages I must give credit where it is due. The title of this chapter comes directly from the scene in the heart-warming movie *My Big Fat Greek Wedding*, when the bride-to-be introduces her vegetarian fiancé to her mother. The mother reacts to this news with disbelief and horror before quickly regaining her composure and reassuring her future son-in-law that it's perfectly okay if he doesn't eat meat, because she makes lamb. When we first heard these lines, my entire family burst out in the kind of laughter that erupts when the circumstances being portrayed are deeply familiar to you. We all swore that the scriptwriter must have been a fly on the wall in my mom's kitchen any time one of us told her that one of our guests for dinner didn't eat meat. There is simply always, always lamb on the table.

Left: A cafe in the harbor, Muscat, Oman

Jeanne Previte prepares to serve her cabbage rolls.

I think her insistence on serving lamb was more than just stubbornness. Mom and Dad were practically the queen and king of lamb in our area. That's not hyperbole and not only because there really was a Sheep Queen (as well as a Beef Queen, Pig Queen, and so on) named at the Hardin County Fair every year. Years before anyone had ever heard of "getting to know your local farmer" at the market, for instance, Mom had basically cold-called a number of the farmers in the area demanding to know why every time she was on the highways of rural Ohio she passed dozens of sheep grazing on farmland and yet she couldn't find an ounce of decent lamb to cook at the grocery store. All that regular consumers could get their hands on in those days was gamy mutton, which is nothing at all like the sweet lamb that Mom had grown up eating, thanks to the Lebanese butchers in Detroit. Soon enough she'd arranged to buy lambs directly from those farms and have them slaughtered and butchered just for us. And to increase demand for more of this succulent lamb, she would go to the annual fair every year and teach people how to cook it; this was actually a two birds, one stone situation for Mom, since she showcased this lovely, tender lamb in an array of Lebanese dishes that no rural Ohioan had probably ever tasted before they crossed Mom's path.

HARVEST AND HERB

All the way from 'the old country' Previte shares the taste of good sausage at the Harvest & Herb Festival

4A   September 16, 1998

By MELISSA NEWMAN
Ada Herald Staff

Every Friday night at Peter and Jeanne Previte's house there's a special dish. It could be an Italian supper or Lebanese, but the meal leading into the weekend is always meat free. Jeanne has Lebanese ancestors and Peter Italian. Sometimes, they say it's a problem living in the same household and having enough room on the table to allocate to each culture.

It's tradition and memories that drive Peter and Jeanne and when the Harvest & Herb Festival rolls around from year to year, he brings some of those memories to life by sharing his sausage from a recipe straight from the "Old Country," Sicily.

Previte credits his talent for Italian cooking to his Italian-American mother and growing up in an Italian section of New Brunswick, New Jersey.

There were many ethnic festivals held in New Brunswick and one that Previte recalls fondly is the Italian festivals.

"I can remember men grilling fresh Italian sausage on the streets during the festival and making these delicious Italian sausage sandwiches, which included peppers and onions in a tomato sauce on a 'hard' roll," Previte said.

"I can still smell it as I talk to you about it," Previte continues.

Thirteen years ago, Previte started cooking his Italian food at the first Harvest and Herb Festival in downtown Ada.

"When I heard we were going to have a downtown celebration and because we were calling it 'the harvest and herb festival,' I thought this would be an idea way of sharing with the community my ethnic roots," Previte explains.

At its beginning, the festival was geared more towards crafts and according to Previte, festival committee members appeared a little reluctant to include his Italian food concession and when Previte requested two booths for his sausage making, a committee meeting had to be held. When the ladies decided to let Peter go ahead with the sausage booths, later it turned out for the best. Previte's Italian cooking draws many customers.

Previte says it's more than just a booth now, it's a way to socialize with family and friends and a way for them to share good times together.

See, Italian, next page

Previte's Sausage

Enjoy Previte's Homemade Italian Sausage

Boun Appetito!   Come and enjoy it!

Made from an old-world family receipe with all natural ingredients and the finest imported spices.

192

Peter Previte and his daughter Rose greet customers with friendly smiles at their popular Italian sausage stand at festivals.

Not to be outdone, Dad, meanwhile, was for many years the president of the Lamb Improvement Association in Hardin County, an organization dedicated to teaching people how to breed and cook lamb. Once the guys at the association figured out how good Mom was at cooking the meat, they brought her in to do demos for them, too.

So the lamb love runs deep in my family, and I'm not immune. For years no matter where I lived, one of my main objectives, always, was to figure out where I could get the best lamb in the area. In Moscow, my main sources of good lamb were what the expats called the Central Asian markets, or *rynoks* in Russian—so-called because the farmers at the markets sell vegetables from their respective central Asian countries—and a very close friend who was a diplomat at the Australian embassy and thus had access to shipments of great lamb. Until quite recently, it was pretty rough for consumers in the U.S. to get decent lamb unless they lived near a Costco (which consistently had superior lamb for years before other groceries caught on; so kudos to you, lamb buyers of Costco). In recent years, I've become determined to encourage the breeding of the phenomenal Awassi sheep (page 173) in the U.S. As of this writing, there are exactly two farms in the States breeding them, one each in North Carolina and California. It's probably not too surprising to learn that starting my own Awassi sheep farm *is* in fact on my bucket list.

All of that is to say that, whew, lamb isn't just a food to us; it's a true passion. But that is not to take anything away from the other satisfying proteins in this chapter! There is of course beef, and chicken, and duck, and even some fish and seafood. Growing up in the Midwest, we didn't eat any fresh fish at all, so it took me a little while to find seafood dishes that I liked, let alone loved enough to include here. But I did find them! And I hope very much that you will find the recipes as delicious as I do.

Top left: Mom's cooking featured in the local *Ada Herald*, 1985

Bottom left: Showcasing Dad's sausage-making hobby in the *Ada Herald*, 1998

Above: Dad and I in the *Ada Herald*, 1988

IN THIS CHAPTER

Above: Christina and I lunching in Lebanon

Top right: Fish market, Muscat, Oman

Bottom right: Kibbeh Nayeh in the world

Kibbeh Nayeh
Ground Raw Lamb with Bulgur

Makes 8 to 12 servings

Above: Preparing rose petals to make kibbeh

My mom learned how to make kibbeh nayeh from her own mother, who came from the west Beqaa region in Lebanon. Mom typically uses little to no spice, so that the full flavor of the lamb comes through. If you're a fan of dishes like carpaccio, sashimi, and tartare, this will blow your mind. To the uninitiated it might seem like this is a pretty straightforward dish to make. But that is definitely not the case. Even in my mom's own family, among her sisters and cousins, battle lines are drawn in an instant if someone chooses the wrong side in debates about the bulgur-to-meat ratio, amount and proportion of individual spices, or whether rose petals are in or out. One constant, no matter which side you're on, is that everyone is careful not to let the meat get too warm. Some joke that the Christian Lebanese serve their kibbeh nayeh with the sign of the cross pressed into the surface to give thanks for the food, and also as a little prayer that it doesn't kill anyone. If you order your lamb from a Lebanese butcher counter, it's fine to have them grind it. If not, it's better to get a bone-in leg and grind it yourself; Mom would definitely approve.

In 2019, I traveled to northern Lebanon with two of my aunts to visit my maternal grandfather's village. There we were delighted to meet some distant cousins. The very first dish we had with them was kibbeh nayeh. It felt so appropriate to all of us, as we, too, back in Ohio and Michigan, have always served it for special occasions. One big surprise, however, was that my cousins served the kibbeh with harissa (page 35), though they had not heard the word and did not know that it's a staple in Tunisia and Morocco. The meal and that moment has stayed with me as an example of the many threads that tie the people and customs of these vast lands together, even as the countries in the region are often at odds, and even war. Lebanon has always been a safe place for refugees; the country has taken in so many evacuees from conflict, and the food shows it. Somebody from North Africa likely came to this tiny village at some point and taught someone how to make harissa, and now everyone here serves it with their kibbeh nayeh!

During our visit, I bought some kamouneh, which is the spice mix they grind and use for their kibbeh. While eating their kibbeh with harissa is to be unique to them, this spice mix is more universal, and seems similar to the spices we had in the kibbeh throughout the country. When I returned home, I asked a friend to translate the label on the package and poured the mixture onto a baking sheet to individually identify each spice and herb. Then we reverse engineered the mixture, which complements the lamb (or goat) beautifully for those who appreciate spice more than Mom does.

For the kibbeh seasoning (optional):

1 tablespoon ground allspice

1 tablespoon ground cinnamon

1 tablespoon ground cumin

1 tablespoon ground dried rose petals

1 tablespoon dried mint leaves

1 tablespoon dried marjoram

1 cup (140 g) fine bulgur wheat

1 medium onion

2 pounds (910 g) boneless leg of lamb, finely ground

1¾ tablespoons kosher salt, plus more as needed

Freshly ground black pepper

For serving:

Extra-virgin olive oil, preferably Lebanese unfiltered

Harissa (page 35; optional)

White onion, sliced

Fresh herbs, such as mint (optional)

Pita

To make the optional kibbeh seasoning, in a small bowl mix together the allspice, cinnamon, cumin, rose petals, mint, and marjoram. Set aside until needed or store in a tightly covered container in a cool, dark place up to 6 months.

Place the bulgur wheat in a medium bowl and add cold water to cover by about 2 inches (5 cm). Let stand for 30 minutes. Drain through a fine-mesh strainer, and then squeeze it to release as much of the water as possible.

Meanwhile, grate the onion on the fine teeth of a box grater.

In a large bowl, mix the onion and up to 2 tablespoons kibbeh seasoning, if using, with the ground lamb. Add the drained bulgur, the salt, and pepper to taste. Knead until well combined and softened, dipping your hands in ice water to cool them down if they get too warm; this may take several minutes.

Pat the mixture into an oblong or round shape, depending on the shape of your serving plate. Transfer to the plate and decorate the surface with the tines of a fork or the bowl of a spoon if desired.

If not eating at once, place in the refrigerator until serving (and once served, put the kibbeh nayeh back in the fridge after it's been out for an hour or two).

Serve with olive oil, harissa, if using, sliced onion, fresh herbs, if using, and pita.

Kibbeh Sanieh
Baked Ground Lamb with Bulgur

Serves 12 to 16

For the kibbeh:
3 cups (420 g) fine bulgur wheat

2 medium onions

2 pounds (910 g) ground lean lamb, beef, or a combination

1 teaspoon kosher salt

½ teaspoon freshly ground black pepper

¼ teaspoon ground allspice

¼ teaspoon ground cinnamon, nutmeg, cloves, or cumin

For the filling:
2 tablespoons unsalted butter

½ cup (65 g) pine nuts

1 pound (454 g) ground lamb or beef

4 medium onions, finely chopped

1 teaspoon kosher salt

½ teaspoon freshly ground black pepper

⅛ teaspoon ground cinnamon or allspice (optional)

¾ cup (180 ml) extra-virgin olive oil, preferably Lebanese unfiltered, or melted clarified butter, plus more for greasing the pan

In my family we refer to a mixture of butter, lamb, onion, and pine nuts as *hashwee*, and it is at the base of many of our favorite dishes, like Sitti's Syrian Rice (page 144), and this one, which Mom called "Mediterranean Meatloaf" on her restaurant menu. Whenever she made this dish, she'd make a little extra hashwee and serve it the next morning with scrambled eggs. This is a practice I heartily endorse, though I'm personally partial to serving warmed hashwee on top of hummus (page 51) and calling it a meal. Definitely adjust the cinnamon and other warm spices here to your taste; in Lebanon they tend to use more cinnamon in savory dishes than we do in the U.S.

To make the kibbeh, place the bulgur wheat in a medium bowl and add cold water to cover by about 2 inches (5 cm). Let stand for 30 minutes. Drain through a fine-mesh strainer, and then squeeze it to release as much of the water as possible.

Meanwhile, grate the onions on the fine teeth of a box grater.

In a large bowl, mix the onions with the ground lamb. Add the drained bulgur, salt, pepper, allspice, and cinnamon. Knead until well combined and softened, dipping your hands in ice water if necessary to cool them down; this may take several minutes. Set aside.

To make the filling, in a skillet melt the butter over medium heat. Add the pine nuts and cook, stirring, until lightly browned and fragrant. Add the meat, onions, salt, pepper, and cinnamon, if using, and sauté until the meat has lost its pink color and the onion is softened, 10 to 12 minutes. Remove from the heat and set aside.

Preheat the oven to 400°F (205°C). Grease a 17 by 11½-inch (43 by 29 cm) baking pan.

Spread one-half of the kibbeh in the prepared baking pan. Spread the filling evenly over this layer, patting down lightly. Cover the filling with the remaining half of the kibbeh. Dip your hand in ice water and smooth the surface.

Cut the kibbeh into small diamond shapes. Loosen the edges of the kibbeh from the sides of the pan with a knife dipped in ice water. Pour the oil or clarified butter on top of the kibbeh by the spoonful, being sure to cover the entire surface.

Bake until lightly browned, 35 to 40 minutes. Store leftovers in an airtight container in the refrigerator up to 1 week.

Maydān's Lamb Shoulder with Syrian Seven Spice

Serves 8 to 10

⅓ cup (80 g) kosher salt

½ cup (110 g) packed light brown sugar

1 bone-in lamb shoulder (4½ to 5 ½ pounds / 2 to 2.5 kg) or boneless lamb shoulder (3 to 4 pounds/1.4 to 1.8 kg), tied

½ cup (48 g) Syrian Seven Spice (page 173)

For serving:
2 cups (720 ml) Sumac Onion and Herb Salad (page 79)

Flatbread

Labne with Dried Mint (page 49)

Toum (page 34) and/or your preferred sauce

Equipment: Cryo-vac or zip-top bag; sous vide circulator (optional)

The flavor of this shoulder is so divine that I simply can't apologize about the amount of time it takes to prepare; it's worth every second. When we serve this at Maydān it feels like an event. After they are cooked sous vide the shoulders are tied up and hung above the fire where over the next several hours their spiced outsides are transformed into a flavorful crust around the meltingly tender meat (you can see them on page 166). We present the entire bone-in shoulder piled high with sumac onions and herbs and all the sauces (I'll add a shout-out here that I think the labne with dried mint and toum are the two absolute must-haves with this). And this is definitely the moment to serve lots of flatbread for you and your guests to use as your utensils so that you can concoct as many individual bakouns (see page 29) as you can eat!

Leftovers are just as delicious as the main event; two of our favorite next-day dishes are the pulled lamb served on top of creamy hummus (page 51), or rolled in flatbread with shatta and pickles and whatever else sounds good to you.

Combine the salt and sugar. Rub the mixture on the lamb shoulder and place in the refrigerator for at least 30 minutes and up to 3 hours.

Rinse the shoulder under cold water and pat it dry. Rub all over with the seven spice.

Place the lamb in a cryo-vac or zip-top bag. Sous vide at 200°F (90°C) for 18 hours. (Alternatively, place the lamb in a baking dish, cover the pan tightly with aluminum foil, and roast in a 275°F (135°C) oven until very tender when pierced with a fork, about 8 hours.)

Remove the bag from the water or the baking dish from the oven and let stand until cool enough to handle.

Meanwhile prepare a hot grill.

Remove the shoulder from the baking dish or the bag, pat it dry, and grill on all sides until the outside is seared and crisped.

Place on a platter. Top with Sumac Onion and Herb Salad. Serve with flatbread and your favorite sauces.

Lamb Chakapuli

Georgian Braised Lamb Stew with Tarragon

Serves 6

2¼ pounds (1 kg) boneless lamb shoulder, cut into 2- to 3-inch (5 to 7.5 cm) pieces

1 bottle (750 ml) dry white wine

Kosher salt

2 large onions, chopped

Leaves from 7 ounces (200 g) fresh tarragon stems, very coarsely chopped

2 bunches cilantro, leaves and tender stems, finely chopped

½ to 1 bunch flat-leaf parsley, finely chopped (optional)

1 bunch spring onions, white and green parts, finely chopped

Up to 1 serrano pepper, seeds and ribs removed, finely chopped

1 cup (240 ml) tkemali sauce (sour plum sauce, see Note)

The simplicity of this stew is belied by its flavor, which is defined by the prodigious amount of fresh tarragon. Until I had chakapuli in Georgia, it had never occurred to me that all a homestyle lamb stew needed to be extraordinary was a bushel of tarragon (yes, I'm exaggerating, but only a little). This is a time to use tarragon from your backyard or to procure it at a farmers' market; you'd need a shopping cart full of those tiny little packs that hang in many produce departments to achieve the amount you need here. Don't let it scare you away, though. Tarragon and lamb are a match made in heaven and this recipe is the path to paradise. This recipe is another from my dear friend Mamuka (see page 88), whose generous spirit abounds, as does his enthusiasm for sharing the culture of his country.

Put the lamb in a large pot and add the wine and a couple of pinches of salt. Bring to a boil over medium heat. Reduce the heat and simmer for 15 minutes, stirring occasionally. Add the onion and simmer for 10 minutes.

Add the tarragon, cilantro, parsley, if using, spring onions, serrano, tkemali sauce, and 4 cups (960 ml) water and stir to combine. Bring to a boil, then cover the pot, reduce the heat to a simmer, and cook until the lamb is very tender, 1 to 1½ hours.

Taste and adjust the salt if necessary. Serve hot.

Note: Tkemali sauce is made from the sour plums that are a major component of Georgian cooking. I've never seen the equivalent in fresh sour plums here, but bottled tkemali sauce can be found at Georgian and Russian markets and online. It adds a sour and sweet flavor that really brightens this dish and wherever it's added.

Khinkali
Georgian Meat-Filled Dumplings

Makes about 24 dumplings;
serves 4 to 6

For the dough:

4 cups (500 g) all-purpose flour, plus more
for kneading and rolling out the dough

2 teaspoons kosher salt

2 large eggs

1 cup (240 ml) lukewarm water (about
110°F/45°C)

For the filling:

8 ounces (225 g) 80/20 ground beef

8 ounces (225 g) ground pork (not too lean,
if possible)

1 medium onion, finely chopped

2 cloves garlic, finely chopped

1 bunch fresh cilantro, leaves and tender stems,
finely chopped

¼ cup (½ stick / 55 g) unsalted butter, melted
and cooled

2 teaspoons kosher salt

¾ teaspoon caraway seed, ground

¾ teaspoon coriander seed, ground

½ teaspoon freshly ground black pepper,
plus more for serving

¼ teaspoon cayenne pepper

Since my first bite of these little dumplings, I've been a devoted fan. I even took a class in the mountains of Georgia dedicated solely to making them, though I will probably never achieve the nineteen individual pleats on each dumpling that many insist are de rigueur. Serve these with lots of freshly ground black pepper, and to do it the Georgian way, instruct everyone to bite the dumplings off the little dough hat at the top of each one, and leave the hats behind. The winner is whoever has the most hats, and an excellent prize is a box of leftover khinkali that they can fry in butter for breakfast the following morning.

To make the dough, in a large bowl, whisk together the flour and salt. Make a hole in the center of the flour and add the eggs. Use a fork to beat the eggs; it's fine if some flour gets mixed in with them.

Continue to beat with the fork while you pour in the warm water and combine it with the eggs. Stir with a wooden spoon, combining more flour into the liquid with every stroke until a dough forms; turn it out onto a lightly floured work surface and knead until the dough is smooth and elastic. Place the dough in a lightly oiled bowl, cover with plastic wrap, and set aside while you make the filling.

To make the filling, in a large bowl, place the beef, pork, onion, garlic, cilantro, butter, salt, caraway, coriander, black pepper, cayenne pepper, and 1½ cups (360 ml) water. Use your hands or a spatula to mix just until combined; don't overmix.

On a lightly floured work surface, divide the dough into 3 equal pieces and roll each of them into a ball; keep them covered with plastic wrap while you work. Set a parchment-lined baking sheet nearby and lightly dust it with flour.

Working with one ball at a time, roll the dough out ¼ inch (6 mm) thick. Using a 2-inch (5-cm) round cutter, cut out 8 rounds, rerolling and cutting scraps as necessary (you'll have about 24 rounds total).

Roll out each dough round to a 4- to 5-inch (10- to 12-cm) round. Place about 1 tablespoon filling in the center and pleat the dough edge all the way around to enclose the filling. Pinch the pleats together to seal and gently twist the top to seal the filling inside. Place the khinkali on the floured parchment paper and cover loosely with plastic wrap. Continue with the remaining rounds and filling, and then with all the remaining dough balls and filling.

Bring a large pot of generously salted water to a boil over high heat. Add several khinkali to the water and stir carefully to make sure they aren't sticking to the bottom of the pot. Boil gently until the meat is cooked and the dough is al dente, 5 to 7 minutes.

Use a spider to transfer the cooked khinkali to paper towels and keep warm. Continue until all the khinkali are cooked.

Serve hot with plenty of black pepper.

Ribeye with Georgian Dry Rub

Serves 2

1 tablespoon ground blue fenugreek

2 teaspoons gochugaru (Korean red chili flakes) or 1½ teaspoons Aleppo pepper flakes

1 (16-ounce / 455-g) bone-in ribeye steak, at least 1½ inches (4 cm) thick

Vegetable oil, for the grill

1 tablespoon kosher salt

The lovely republic of Georgia is the inspiration for so much of what I do in my restaurants, at home, and here in this book. The way this ribeye came to be is just one example of the magic that happens in the wake of Georgian hospitality. As part of our "cooking with grandmas" research trip before opening Maydān, we stayed with friends in a small village in mountainous western Georgia. When we'd made the arrangements, we had no idea that our visit was going to overlap with their hosting a very large wedding anniversary party. Mortified, we tried to make plans to be elsewhere during the event, but our hosts would not have it. Reluctantly we agreed, but only if they allowed us to cook something for the party. Off they went to find us some meat while we built a fire for cooking. When they returned, they proudly presented something they were sure would thrill us Americans: a beef ribeye. It was an exquisitely gracious gesture, and we were touched and eager to match their enthusiasm with a finished dish that would demonstrate our gratitude to be included in this special event. However, this meat was nothing like the bright red, beautifully marbled ribeye from home, and it definitely hadn't been stored in a refrigerator. We began to worry that making the ribeye palatable might be too tall an order. With a bit of digging through our hosts' spice collection, we found salvation: blue fenugreek. Unique to Georgia, blue fenugreek is related to the Indian fenugreek more common here in the U.S., but it has a sweeter, warmer aroma and flavor. We mixed up a simple dry rub of blue fenugreek and adjika (ground dried chile, see Note on page 213) and massaged it into the ribeye then put the seasoned meat over the fire. The result was rich, delicious, and positively transporting. This rub is excellent on all sorts of cuts of meat, including rugged Georgian mountain cow.

In a small dish, stir together the blue fenugreek and gochugaru.

Two to twenty-four hours before you start cooking, pat the steak dry and rub on the fenugreek and gochugaru blend. Place, uncovered, in the refrigerator.

When ready to cook, prepare a hot grill and oil the grate.

Thirty minutes before cooking the steak, remove it from the refrigerator and place it at room temperature. Season both sides generously with kosher salt.

Grill the steak for 5 to 6 minutes on each side, or until an instant-read thermometer reads 120°F (49°C).

Remove the steak from the grill and let it rest for at least 6 to 8 minutes. Slice against the grain ¼ inch (6 mm) thick and serve.

Ras el Hanout–Rubbed Duck Breast

Serves 2

2 boneless duck breasts (7 to 8 ounces / 200 to 225 g each), trimmed of any extra outer fat

4 teaspoons ras el hanout

2 teaspoons kosher salt

Flaky sea salt (such as Maldon), for serving

Sweet Tomato Jam (page 39), for serving

Equipment: Cryo-vac or zip-top bag; sous vide circulator

It used to be that the best, and maybe even the only, way to enjoy duck breast was when it was prepared by a skilled chef in a restaurant kitchen. Then sous vide circulators became more commonplace, and now the secret to those chefs' success is available to all of us. And that secret is cooking the seasoned duck sous vide until the meat is exactly medium-rare and then slowly and gently rendering the fat just under its skin while simultaneously browning it to crispy perfection.

Rub the meaty side of the breasts with ras el hanout.

Place the duck breasts in a cryo-vac or zip-top bag. Sous vide at 130°F (55°C) for at least 45 minutes and up to 4 hours.

Take the duck breasts out of the bag and dry them thoroughly with paper towels. If not finishing immediately, place the duck breasts on a cooling rack in the refrigerator up to overnight.

About 30 minutes before finishing, set the breasts on the counter to come to room temperature. Season both sides of the breasts with kosher salt.

Place the breasts skin side down in a cast-iron pan over medium-low heat. Cook until well browned, about 20 minutes, spooning off the rendered fat as it accumulates.

Increase the heat to medium and flip the breasts over. Cook for 1 to 2 minutes, just to sear the meaty side; an instant read thermometer should read 130°F (55°C) for medium-rare. Transfer the breasts to a cutting board, placing them skin side up, and let rest for 5 to 7 minutes.

To serve, cut each breast crosswise into about 8 slices and arrange the slices on plates or a platter. Sprinkle with flaky salt, and serve with the sweet tomato jam.

Roasted Turmeric Chicken

Serves 4

1 roasting chicken (about 4 pounds / 1.8 kg)

For the turmeric brine:
1 small onion, quartered

1 head garlic, cut in half crosswise through the equator

½ cup (70 g) ground turmeric

¼ cup (16 g) whole coriander seed, crushed with mortar and pestle or very coarsely ground

¼ cup (70 g) kosher salt

2 tablespoons sugar

1 tablespoon whole cardamom pods, very coarsely ground

1 cinnamon stick (3 inches / 7.5 cm), cracked in several pieces

For the turmeric paste:
6 tablespoons (90 ml) grapeseed oil

2 tablespoons extra-virgin olive oil, preferably Lebanese unfiltered

Scant ½ cup (30 g) whole coriander seed, ground

1 tablespoon ground turmeric

8 cloves garlic, finely chopped with kosher salt (see Note)

1 tablespoon kosher salt

Toum (page 34), for serving

Flatbread, for serving

The generous amount of turmeric used here gives this chicken a vibrant yellow color and bursting flavor to match. At Maydān, we present the whole chicken to the table, plated on top of our Toné bread to absorb every drop of scrumptious juice, with a bowl of toum to brighten each bite with a burst of garlicky goodness. This dish was inspired by the delectable chickens we've eaten at Barbar, a fun and energetic 24/7 restaurant in Beirut, and on the sides of many roads in Morocco and Tunisia.

To spatchcock the chicken for even roasting, place it breast side down on a cutting board. Starting at the neck end, use poultry shears or a sharp boning knife to cut along one side of the backbone toward the tail, stopping your cut about two-thirds of the way down the length of the backbone. Repeat on the other side of the backbone. Now cut down the last bit of length on either side to completely remove the backbone.

Flip the chicken over and press down hard on the center of the breast to make it lie flat. Tuck the wing tips under the wing bone.

To make the brine, in a large bowl or other container that is large enough to hold the chicken, place the onion, garlic, turmeric, coriander, salt, sugar, cardamom, cinnamon, and 4½ cups (1 liter) water. Stir together until the salt and sugar are dissolved. Add the chicken (you can fold it back into a compact shape so it fits more easily if necessary).

Brine the chicken in the refrigerator for at least 1 hour and up to 24 hours.

To make the paste, in a blender combine the oils, coriander, turmeric, garlic, and salt. Blend until well combined. Refrigerate until needed.

Remove the chicken from the brine. Discard the brine and pat the chicken dry with a towel.

Rub the turmeric paste all over the chicken and let stand at room temperature while the oven heats (if not roasting right away, place the chicken uncovered in the refrigerator for up to 12 hours).

Preheat the oven to 450°F (230°C).

Place the flattened chicken, breast side up, on a rack in a roasting pan. Roast for 15 minutes. Reduce the oven temperature to 325°F (165°C) and roast until the juices run clear when the thickest part of the thigh is pierced with a sharp knife, 35 to 45 minutes.

Let stand for 10 minutes. Cut into 8 pieces and serve with toum and flatbread to soak up the juices.

Note: Chop the garlic, then sprinkle about ½ teaspoon of the salt on top, and continue to chop it very fine. When adding it to the other ingredients, scrape it and any juices into the bowl together.

Chicken Satsivi
Chicken in Walnut Sauce

Serves 6 to 8

1 chicken (about 4 pounds / 1.8 kg), whole or cut into pieces

Kosher salt

¼ cup (½ stick / 55 g) unsalted butter

2 medium onions, finely chopped

8 cups (910 g) walnuts

1 tablespoon blue fenugreek

½ teaspoon ground cloves

½ teaspoon ground cinnamon

½ teaspoon ground coriander

¼ teaspoon crushed saffron threads

2 cloves garlic, crushed with a garlic press

¼ teaspoon cayenne pepper, plus more as needed

Adjika (Georgian red pepper sauce), for serving (see Note)

Tkemali sauce (sour plum sauce, see Note on page 203), for serving (optional)

This dish always transports me right back to the night I first encountered Georgian food prepared by a lovely cook in Moscow (see page 12). The sight and smell of all the walnuts she chopped reminded me of home, but this dish was like nothing I had tasted before. I don't know what alchemy turns finely ground walnuts into the creamiest (cream-free!) sauce I've ever had, but I'm so glad my Georgian friend Mamuka (see page 88) was willing to share this recipe.

Place the chicken in a large pot and cover with water by 3 inches. Season the water generously with several pinches of salt. Bring the water to a boil. Reduce the heat and simmer until the chicken is cooked through and an instant-read thermometer inserted in the meatiest part of the thigh registers at least 180°F (80°C), 35 to 45 minutes. Strain the chicken and reserve the broth separately. Place the chicken on a cutting board.

Set a broiler rack 6 inches (14 cm) below the heat source and set the broiler to high. Cut the cooled chicken into 8 pieces (unless it is already cut up) and arrange the pieces skin side up on a baking sheet. Sprinkle all over with salt. Broil until browned, 8 to 10 minutes. Remove from the heat and set aside.

Meanwhile, to prepare the walnut sauce, melt the butter in a skillet over medium heat. Add the onions and a couple of pinches of salt and cook, stirring, until translucent and softened, about 8 minutes. Remove from the heat and set aside.

Process the walnuts in a food processor until very finely chopped. Transfer the nuts to a large bowl. Add the blue fenugreek, cloves, cinnamon, coriander, saffron, garlic, cayenne, and 1 teaspoon salt. Use your hands to knead and rub the walnuts until they are very oily and stick firmly together when pressed between your fingers; this will take about 20 minutes.

Add the sautéed onions and about 1 cup (240 ml) of the reserved broth to the walnuts and stir until the mixture takes on the consistency of sour cream; the color will lighten considerably. Add more broth as necessary to loosen the walnuts.

Whisk enough broth into the walnut mixture to make it pourable, and pour it into the large pot. Bring to a boil and simmer for 10 minutes. Add the pieces of chicken. Return to a boil, then reduce the heat and simmer if necessary to reheat the chicken. Remove from the heat.

Serve hot, and pass the adjika and tkemali sauce, if using, separately at the table.

Note: The term adjika refers both to a red pepper powder that is similar to paprika and a hot red pepper sauce, which is what I'm referring to here. Both forms of adjika can be found at stores that carry Georgian and Armenian items, and online.

Sayadieh
Grilled "Fisherman's Catch" with
Chermoula and Tahina

Serves 6 to 8

⅔ cup (165 ml) extra-virgin olive oil, preferably Lebanese unfiltered

6 tablespoons (90 ml) fresh lemon juice (from about 2 lemons)

2 cups (220 g) chopped red onion

4 cloves garlic, chopped

¼ cup (10 g) finely chopped fresh cilantro

2 teaspoons sweet paprika

2 teaspoons kosher salt

1 teaspoon ground turmeric

1 teaspoon freshly ground black pepper

1 teaspoon Aleppo pepper flakes

2 pounds (910 g) skin-on sea bass or other white fish fillets

Vegetable oil, for the grill

For serving:
Chermoula (page 36)

Tahina (page 34)

Fresh cilantro leaves

A quick dip in a flavorful marinade is all most white fish fillets need to make them ready for grilling. The smokiness added by this method of cooking really complements and enhances the saffron in the chermoula, which itself mixes with the tahina into a creamy, perfectly savory accompaniment. At Maydān we make this with whatever white fish our fish suppliers tell us are best when we're buying (our own kind of "fisherman's catch"). I especially like any kind of sea bass cooked this way.

To make the marinade, in a medium bowl combine the olive oil, lemon juice, onion, garlic, cilantro, paprika, salt, turmeric, black pepper, and Aleppo pepper flakes. Stir together until well blended.

Put the fish in a baking dish or other container just big enough to hold it all. Add the marinade and turn the fish over several times to make sure it is thoroughly coated. Refrigerate for 30 to 60 minutes.

Prepare a hot grill.

Lightly grease the grill grate with oil and add the fish skin side down. Partially cover the grill and grill until the fish is cooked through and flaky, about 7 minutes.

Transfer to a serving platter skin side up. Drizzle with the chermoula and tahina and garnish with cilantro. Serve, passing more chermoula and tahina in bowls at the table.

Roasted Whole Fish with Spicy Cabbage

Serves 4

For the spicy cabbage:

1¾ cups (165 g) shredded green cabbage

½ cup (45 g) thinly sliced fennel

½ cup (120 ml) Chermoula (page 36)

½ cup (120 ml) Sumac Onions (page 79)

Kosher salt

For the fish:

2- to 3-pound (910 g to 1.4 kg) whole dourade or branzino, cleaned and scaled

2 tablespoons Red Shatta (page 38)

2 tablespoons ground cumin

2 tablespoons ground sumac

2 tablespoons kosher salt, plus more for the radishes

1 orange, cut into half-moon slices

½ bunch fresh cilantro

½ bunch fresh parsley

1 bunch radishes, tops trimmed to 1 to 2 inches (2.5 to 5 cm), cut in half if large

Extra-virgin olive oil, preferably Lebanese unfiltered, for the radishes and for serving

For serving:

1 cup Sumac Onion and Herb Salad (page 79)

Chermoula (page 36)

Flaky sea salt (such as Maldon), for sprinkling

Lemon wedges

Roasting is one of my favorite ways to prepare fish at home, because there's no need to flip or fuss with the fish while it cooks. Just a few simple touches beforehand, and you can put it in the oven and pretty much forget about it until it's ready. Putting some radishes on the baking sheet to roast along with the fish and mixing some sliced cabbage and fennel with a bit of smoky, saffron-y chermoula (just one more of so many reasons to always have this sauce on hand) provide two beautiful and unusual accompaniments.

To make the spicy cabbage, in a large bowl place the cabbage, fennel, chermoula, sumac onions, and a pinch of salt. Toss until well coated. Refrigerate for at least 20 minutes and up to 4 days. Taste before serving and adjust the salt if necessary.

Position a rack in the center of the oven and preheat the oven to 400°F (205°C). Line a rimmed baking sheet with parchment paper.

To make the fish, place them on the lined baking sheet. Liberally rub the fish on the inside with the shatta and generously sprinkle the outside with the cumin, sumac, and salt. Place 3 to 4 half-moon slices of orange along with a few sprigs of cilantro and parsley in the belly cavity of each fish.

In a small bowl, toss the radishes with a drizzle of olive oil and a few pinches salt. Arrange them on the baking sheet around the fish.

Roast until the fish is flaky or until an instant-read thermometer inserted into the thickest part of the fish reads 135°F (60°C), 20 to 30 minutes, depending on the size and thickness of the fish.

Remove the fish and radishes from the oven and then remove the oranges, cilantro, and parsley from the fish and discard. Arrange the fish and radishes on a platter and place the spicy cabbage alongside. Garnish with the sumac onion and herb salad. Drizzle with chermoula and olive oil and sprinkle with flaky salt. Serve with lemon wedges.

Balik Ekmek

Mackerel Sandwiches

Serves 4

4 skin-on mackerel fillets (6 to 8 ounces /
170 to 225 g each)

Kosher salt and freshly ground black pepper

Extra-virgin olive oil, preferably Lebanese
unfiltered

4 hoagie rolls

1 ripe tomato, sliced

2 cups (110 g) shredded romaine lettuce

Red wine vinegar

Lemon Mayonnaise (recipe follows)

Harissa (optional; page 35)

The city of Istanbul is on the banks of the Bosporus Strait, and under one of the main bridges fishermen pull fish out of the water and grill and fry them on the spot to sell in sandwiches. One of my favorite memories is getting these balik ekmek sandwiches right off the boats. When I returned to the States and we began recreating these sandwiches at Compass Rose, we realized they needed a little heat, and that's where the very inauthentic but quite delicious harissa came in.

Lightly season the mackerel fillets with salt and pepper. Set a platter lined with paper towels next to the stovetop. In a large cast-iron skillet, heat 2 tablespoons olive oil over medium heat until shimmering. Add the mackerel fillets skin side down. Cook until the skin is golden brown and the fillets release easily from the pan, 5 to 8 minutes.

Flip the fish and cook on the other side just until opaque, 30 seconds to 1 minute. Transfer the fillets to the paper towels and set aside. If necessary, repeat with the remaining mackerel fillets, using more oil if necessary

Meanwhile, toast the hoagie rolls in a toaster oven or under the broiler.

Spread the tomatoes on a plate and put the lettuce in a bowl. Drizzle both with some olive oil and vinegar and lightly season with salt and pepper. Toss the lettuce to lightly coat.

To assemble the sandwiches, spread 1 to 2 tablespoons lemon mayonnaise on the bottom half of each roll. Place one fillet skin side up on each. Top the fish with tomato and lettuce.

If desired, spread some harissa on the top half of the rolls. Place the tops on the sandwiches and serve.

Lemon Mayonnaise

Makes 1½ cups (360 ml)

***

1 cup (240 ml) grapeseed oil

⅓ cup (75 ml) extra-virgin olive oil, preferably
Lebanese unfiltered

1 large egg yolk

1½ tablespoons fresh lemon juice

½ teaspoon kosher salt, plus more to taste

Grated zest of 1 lemon

Grated zest of 1 lime (optional)

Grated zest of 1 orange (optional)

Pour the grapeseed and olive oils into a 2-cup (480 ml) glass measuring cup and set aside.

Place the egg yolk, lemon juice, and salt in a food processor and process to blend.

With the processor running, slowly add the oil in a light stream until the sauce is emulsified and creamy; you may not need all of the oil. Add the lemon zest and the lime and orange zest, if using. Pulse once or twice to combine.

Store the mayonnaise in an airtight container in the refrigerator up to 1 week.

Octopus, Two Ways

Serves 2

Juice of 1 lemon

2 pounds (910 g) raw octopus tentacles

When we traveled to Tunisia before opening Maydān, a friend who worked for the Institute for War and Peace Reporting introduced us to her lovely parents, who invited us to cook with them at their home in the beautiful coastal town of Sidi Bou Said. Our friend's mother grew up on the Kerkennah Islands, located about 13 miles (20 km) off the coast of Sfax, and she very much wanted to show us how to prepare octopus the Kerkennaise way. We were more than happy to oblige. She began by boiling the octopus for 30 minutes in water acidulated with lemon juice, which helps preserve the octopus's natural color and puts it well on its way to tender. And then she divided up the tentacles and made two distinct and very tasty dishes that go beautifully together.

One was an octopus salad made of thinly sliced tentacles that were simmered in a shallow bath of olive oil and vinegar until very lightly browned. Then the sauce and octopus were spooned over a platter of freshly sliced tomatoes and onion and topped with fresh parsley and sliced lemon. The simplicity belies the incredible flavor, both of the octopus itself and the fragrant cooking liquid that becomes the warm dressing. The other dish was a specialty of her home islands, and it is named accordingly. Always served with seafood, sauce Kerkennaise is popular throughout Tunisia. In this version, the tomato-based sauce isn't just an accompaniment; the sliced octopus tentacles are simmered in it until the pieces are perfectly tender and the garlicky sauce is redolent with the aroma and flavor of the sweet octopus. Though either dish can of course be eaten on its own, serving them at a single meal is nicely efficient and reaches another level of deliciousness.

Bring a large pot of water to a boil. Add the lemon juice and the octopus tentacles. Cover and bring back to a boil. Boil gently for 30 minutes.

Drain and set aside until cool enough to handle.

[recipes continues]

Tunisian Octopus Salad

Serves 2

***

½ cup (120 ml) extra-virgin olive oil, preferably Lebanese unfiltered

¼ cup (60 ml) white wine vinegar

½ of the octopus tentacles (recipe on page 220), sliced crosswise ⅜ inch (1 cm) thick

Kosher salt and freshly ground black pepper

1 large heirloom tomato or 2 to 3 Campari tomatoes

½ sweet onion, thinly sliced

1 lemon, sliced into 8 wedges

½ bunch fresh flat-leaf parsley, coarsely chopped

***

Pour the olive oil and vinegar into a sauté pan. Add the sliced octopus to the pan, arranging the pieces in a single layer. Season with salt and pepper. Bring the liquid to a gentle simmer over medium heat. Simmer until the octopus is tender and lightly browned, 20 to 30 minutes.

Meanwhile, arrange the tomato and onion on a serving platter.

Spoon the cooked octopus tentacles and all the cooking liquid onto the tomatoes and onions. Place the lemon wedges around the platter, sprinkle with parsley, and serve.

Octopus with Sauce Kerkennaise

Serves 2

***

1 pound (455 g) plum tomatoes, chopped

1 large onion, chopped

3 cloves garlic, chopped

Kosher salt

¼ cup (60 ml) extra-virgin olive oil, preferably Lebanese unfiltered

2 tablespoons tomato paste

¾ teaspoon sweet paprika

¾ teaspoon ground cumin

¾ teaspoon ground coriander

¾ teaspoon caraway seed, ground

¾ teaspoon ground turmeric

¼ teaspoon crushed red pepper, plus more as needed

½ of the octopus tentacles (recipe on page 220), sliced ½ inch (12 mm) thick

1 tablespoon white wine vinegar, plus more as needed

½ cup (25 g) coarsely chopped flat-leaf parsley, for serving

Flaky sea salt (such as Maldon), for serving (optional)

***

Place the tomatoes, onion, garlic, and 1 teaspoon salt in a food processor and pulse until finely chopped. Set aside.

In a sauté pan, heat the oil over medium heat just until warm. Add the tomato paste and cook, stirring, until toasted, about 2 minutes. Push the tomato sauce to the side of the pan, and add the paprika, cumin, coriander, caraway, turmeric, and crushed red pepper; toast until fragrant, 30 to 60 seconds.

Add the chopped tomato mixture, stir everything together, and bring to a simmer. Add the octopus and simmer until the octopus is tender and the flavors are blended, 20 to 45 minutes, depending on the texture of the octopus.

Remove the pan from the heat and stir in the vinegar. Taste and adjust the salt or vinegar.

Serve, topped with parsley and flaky salt.

Compass Rose Cocktail

Sparkling Wine and Pomegranate

Serves 1

Rose water, for the glass

1 ounce (30 ml) pomegranate liqueur, chilled

3 ounces (90 ml) sparkling white wine, chilled

Fresh mint leaf, for garnish

Pomegranate seeds, for garnish

Equipment: Coupe glass

My long experience in bartending prepared me very well to create a cocktail at Compass Rose that would exemplify the spirit of the restaurant. Ruby red pomegranate liqueur and bubbles are a natural pairing and they make a beautiful jewel-toned drink that is entirely appropriate in Compass's softly lit and fabric-draped dining room. The twist here is the rose water, a flavor I love and which is a salute to the extracts my dad and I used to concoct during summer trips to New Jersey using the roses from my grandma Rose's garden. The rose water adds a floral elegance to the drink. I recognize that for some people, however, rose water is an acquired taste. While we used to add the rose water to this cocktail using a small dropper, we now simply give the empty glass a quick spray from an atomizer bottle just before we pour in the drink.

In a coupe glass, pour in a small amount of rose water. Swirl it around the glass, then pour it out; alternatively, put the rose water in a clean, food-safe spritz bottle and spray into the empty glass or on top of the finished cocktail just before adding the garnishes.

Pour the pomegranate liqueur into the glass. Top off with the sparkling wine.

Garnish with a mint leaf and a couple of pomegranate seeds. Serve.

MAYDĀN TAWLE

MAYDĀN TAWLE

In my early plans for Maydān, I didn't intend to have any two-person tables at all. I envisioned all of our guests sitting at long tables and eating family-style. I wanted to bring to life the spirit of the place—the maydān—that had given the restaurant its name. I longed for strangers to come in separately, break bread together at our long tables, and leave as friends, or at least no longer strangers. And to facilitate the bonding, I wanted to forgo everyone having to order food and instead just let the kitchen send out our very best dishes each evening as they were ready. For a long time how people would eat at Maydān felt as important to me as what they would eat, because I believe wholeheartedly that together in a group is simply the best way to eat the food that we serve, like the dishes that are shown here. So much joy comes from sharing food off communal plates—which is safe to do when your utensil is a fresh bite of bread each time—with everyone experimenting with combinations of foods to make each bite.

Ultimately we did not go that route, for there were many voices encouraging me to stick to a more familiar seating model for our guests. I am gratified to see how many of our patrons who first come to us with just one other person will soon return with a bigger group, and I'm happy to say strangers becoming friends does actually happen organically between tables from time to time. One of the many weird things to come out of the tragedy of the Covid era is that it did get us closer to my ideal. The only way we could stay open for a lot of that time was for the kitchen to prepare a pared-down version of our full menu, with foods that all go beautifully together. Everyone paid a single price for food and the kitchen sent it out as it was ready. And even now, in our new normal, we still require large parties to order this way. And we set the best dishes together and send them out as they are ready, just as I imagined long ago.

TAWLE MENU

Mouneh (Pickled Turnips, Cucumbers,
Green Tomatoes), 232

◆

Fattoush (Summer Salad
with Crisped Flatbread), 78

◆

Hummus, Three Ways, 51

◆

Muhammara (Walnut, Roasted
Red Pepper, and Pomegranate Dip), 55

◆

Beef Koobideh
(Persian Minced Beef Kebabs), 174

◆

Shish Taouk (Chicken Kebabs), 182

Grilled Halloumi
with Dukkah and Honey, 232

◆

Sayadieh (Grilled "Fisherman's Catch"
with Chermoula and Tahina), 215

◆

Ribeye with Georgian Dry Rub, 206

◆

Slow-Grilled Cauliflower
with Tahina and Zhough, 97

◆

Maydān's Lamb Shoulder
with Syrian Seven Spice, 200

7

Why Are We All Lactose Intolerant?

Cheese and Dairy

One of the great tragedies of my life is that I cannot comfortably eat dairy, because I love it so very much. That my lactose intolerance didn't present until I was a teenager is no consolation since, when I was a kid, the only dairy I'd eat was mozzarella. I didn't really grow up with much dairy anyway. Most of the adults in my family are lactose intolerant. I know I'm generalizing, but it seems like many people who come from Lebanon and its environs lack the lactase enzyme necessary to digest dairy. And still, there is an impressive array of dairy-based foods from the area. That said, it's in the Caucasus that dairy really holds sway, and Georgia is no exception. Until I spent time there, I'd never dreamed what is possible when an entire country dedicates itself to the endeavor of consuming milk in all forms. Gebjalia, soft cheese rolled with fresh cheese and mint (page 235), is probably the pinnacle of the dairy greatness a nation can achieve. It and the handful of other recipes in this chapter had to pass a very high bar: At one time or another, I threw caution to the wind and ate something that I knew I shouldn't. When I didn't regret my decision, the recipe was deemed worthy enough to share.

Left: Breakfast in Muscat, Oman

IN THIS CHAPTER

Clockwise from top left:
Breakfast at Beit Douma, Lebanon

Jugs for milk, Salala, Oman

Visiting a Bedouin village, Oman

Hadwane Dairy Shop, mountains
outside Beirut

Grilled Halloumi with Dukkah and Honey

Serves 6 to 8

1 package (8.8 ounces / 250 g) halloumi cheese

2 tablespoons grapeseed oil, or as needed

¼ cup (60 ml) clover honey

Dukkah (recipe follows)

Grilled Syrian or Lebanese cheese is a staple in the region, and we created this dish at Maydān to express that tradition. I can never decide which part is more delicious, the warm, melty halloumi cheese or the sweet, nutty topping. We use local-to-us honey and a dukkah blend of peanuts, seeds, and spices that we created especially for this dish. Although we offer this as part of the main tawle meal and many people eat it early in the meal, it can easily be served just before dessert as a sort of cheese plate, or even as the dessert itself.

Slice the halloumi ½ inch (12 mm) thick.

In a large cast-iron pan, heat the grapeseed oil for 1 minute, until very hot. Place the halloumi in the pan (work in batches so as not to crowd the pan) and sear until golden brown on both sides, flipping the slices once, about 90 seconds total.

Transfer the halloumi to a serving platter and keep warm while you sear the rest of the slices. Drizzle over the honey and sprinkle generously with dukkah. Serve at once.

Dukkah

Makes about 2 cups (255 g)

Dukkah is a crunchy and very tasty mixture of nuts, seeds, and spices that originated in Egypt. The exact type and proportion of each of those elements can vary enormously among different blends. The chefs created this one for Maydān specifically to go with our grilled halloumi dish. It's a delicious combination that can be sprinkled on all sorts of things, like peanut butter toast, bread dipped in olive oil, roasted vegetables, and even ice cream.

***

¾ cup (115 g) raw shelled peanuts

½ cup (75 g) white sesame seeds

¼ cup (30 g) black sesame seeds

2 tablespoons coriander seed

2 tablespoons cumin seed

1½ teaspoons black peppercorns

1 tablespoon flaky sea salt (such as Maldon)

***

Preheat the oven to 400°F (205°C).

Spread the peanuts on a rimmed baking sheet. Toast in the oven until they are lightly browned and smell roasty, 5 to 7 minutes, shaking the baking sheet once or twice. Immediately transfer to a plate to cool.

Meanwhile in a cast-iron or other heavy skillet over medium-low heat, toast the white sesame seeds until lightly browned, stirring constantly, about 3 minutes. Transfer them to a small plate to cool.

Return the skillet to the heat and add the black sesame seeds. Toast over medium-low heat, stirring constantly, until they smell toasty and a few have begun to pop, about 3 minutes. Transfer them to the plate with the white sesame seeds to cool.

Return the skillet to the heat and add the coriander. Toast over medium heat, stirring often, until fragrant, about 1 minute. Transfer to a separate small plate to cool.

Repeat with the cumin and peppercorns, transferring each to a separate small dish to cool.

One at a time, grind the coriander, cumin, and black pepper with a mortar and pestle or spice grinder until the spices are well cracked but not completely pulverized.

Transfer the ground spices to a small bowl. Add the toasted sesame seeds.

Grind the peanuts with mortar and pestle; do not pulverize completely, leave them crunchy. Add the peanuts to the bowl.

Add the flaky salt and stir to combine.

Store in an airtight container at room temperature for up to 1 month.

Gebjalia
Georgian Cheese Rolls with Mint

Serves 6 to 8

2 cups (100 g) fresh mint leaves, plus ½ cup (25 g) sliced mint, plus sprigs for garnish

Kosher salt

1 quart (960 ml) milk

1 package (1 pound / 455 g) Sulguni cheese (see Note) or fresh whole-milk mozzarella, cut into thin slices

1 container (1 pound / 455 g) fresh farmer cheese

1 cup (240 ml) labne, or to taste

I'm not sure there is a stronger testament to Georgians' love of dairy than gebjalia, a dish in which cheese is softened in warm milk so that it can be rolled out and stuffed with fresh mint and *another* cheese. The cheese-in-cheese roll is sliced and served in a milk-based sauce. The technique is actually quite straightforward, and the creamy, delicious result defies categorization. As a friend said when she saw it for the first time, "I want to eat all of that, even if I don't really know where or when or how." I'd say that I've usually had it served as an appetizer in Georgia, and when it's served with a green salad and some crusty bread, it makes a superb lunch or a light dinner.

Using a mortar and pestle, pound the 2 cups mint leaves with 1 teaspoon salt until it is pulverized into a purée.

In a medium saucepan, bring the milk just to a boil. Remove the pan from the heat and add the Sulguni. Stir constantly until the cheese is softened and very pliable, like a dough.

Transfer the cheese to a work surface and set the milk aside. Working quickly, use a rolling pin to roll out the cheese into a thin rectangle. Use your hands to rub the mint purée and its liquid all over the surface of the cheese.

Spoon the farmer cheese across the bottom of one long side of the cheese. Starting at that side, roll up the cheese to enclose the farmer cheese. Cover loosely with plastic wrap and set aside while you make the sauce.

Whisk the labne into the reserved milk to make a thick but pourable sauce. You may wish to add more or less labne according to your taste. Stir in the sliced mint. Taste and add salt if necessary.

Slice the cheese roll crosswise about 1 inch (2.5 cm) thick. Arrange the rolls in a shallow serving bowl. Pour over the sauce, garnish with mint, and serve.

Note: Sulguni cheese is a semi-soft cow's milk cheese with a tangy, salty flavor. You can find it in Georgian and Russian grocery stores.

Grilled Cabbage with Turmeric Keshkamel

Serves 4

¼ cup (½ stick / 55 g) unsalted butter

2 tablespoons all-purpose flour

¼ cup (40 g) Kishk (recipe follows or use store-bought)

1½ teaspoons ground turmeric

5 cloves garlic, finely chopped

4 cups (960 ml) milk

Vegetable oil, for the grill

1 large head green cabbage, cut into 6 to 8 wedges

Extra-virgin olive oil, preferably unfiltered Lebanese, for coating the cabbage

Baharat (page 149)

Kosher salt

For serving:
Zhough (page 37)

Flaky sea salt (such as Maldon)

Barberries in verjus, drained (optional, see Note)

Equipment: Rimmed pan that can go on a grill

On one of our trips to Lebanon, cookbook author Bethany Kehdy kindly gave us a tour of some of her favorite places and dishes in Beirut. This is how we learned about kishk, a blend of labne and bulgur wheat that is fermented, dried, and ground. It's a brilliant method of preserving protein- and nutrient-rich yogurt and wheat. Though the practice was undoubtedly prompted by a long-ago need for subsistence, powdered kishk is still a staple in many Lebanese kitchens. It is used as the flavor and thickening base of many soups. After our trip Chef Darnell returned to Maydān's kitchen and had fun playing with the kishk we'd brought back. One of the results was a fantastic mash-up of a classic white sauce (béchamel) and kishk, which he calls "keshkamel." Flavored with garlic and turmeric, the creamy sauce delightfully balances highly seasoned, grilled, and caramelized cabbage. You can order powdered kishk online, or if you'd like to try making your own, see the instructions on the next page.

To make the turmeric keshkamel, in a large saucepan over medium heat, melt the butter. Add the flour, kishk, and turmeric and cook, whisking constantly to prevent lumps, until toasted and fragrant, about 5 minutes.

Add the garlic and sauté about 1 minute. Whisking constantly, slowly pour in the milk and whisk until smooth. Continue to cook over low heat until thickened, 5 to 10 minutes. Remove from the heat and strain into a glass measuring cup. Press a piece of plastic wrap flush against the surface of the sauce and keep warm; set aside.

Prepare a hot two-zone fire in a charcoal grill with a lid: Light a hot fire. When the coals are covered with gray ash, rake them to one side of the grill, creating a cooler zone on the other side to use for indirect cooking. Lightly grease the top grate with oil and put it in place. Put a grill-safe rimmed pan on the cooler (indirect heat) side of the grill.

Meanwhile, make small incisions through the cabbage wedges to make sure they cook all the way through. Brush the cabbage all over with olive oil and season with Baharat and salt.

Place the cabbage wedges on the hot side of the grill and cook until well browned on both cut sides, about 2 minutes per side. Transfer the cabbage to the rimmed pan. Cover the grill, arranging the lid so that the vent is directly over the cabbage; open the vent. Grill, covered, until cooked through, 10 to 15 minutes.

Transfer to a platter or individual plates. Top with the keshkamel, zhough, flaky salt, and soaked barberries, if using, then serve.

Note: This very tasty, tangy garnish is easily made a few days ahead of time. Place ¼ cup (35 g) barberries in a small glass jar with a tight-fitting lid. Pour over enough verjus to cover, tightly cover the jar, and set in the refrigerator for 2 to 3 days, until the barberries are softened, and up to 6 months.

Kishk
Fermented and Preserved Cheese
with Cracked Wheat

Makes 1 pound (455 g)

***

2½ cups (600 ml) labne, plus more as needed

1 cup (175 g) coarse bulgur wheat

2 teaspoons kosher salt

***

In a bowl, mix the labne and the bulgur. Cover the bowl with a kitchen towel and let stand in a cool place for 8 hours.

Add the salt and use your hands to knead the mixture, folding it over itself several times. The mixture should feel moist but not wet, as the bulgur will have absorbed most of the moisture from the labne. If the mixture feels very dry, knead in more labne a spoonful at a time.

Cover the bowl with the kitchen towel and let ferment at room temperature for 24 hours. Fold and turn over the mixture several times. Cover the bowl and let stand for 9 more days, uncovering and folding and kneading every day to prevent mold.

To dry the kishk, spread it out on a rimmed baking sheet and place it in a very low oven (ideally 100°F [40°C]), or spread it on a rack in a dehydrator and heat until dry.

When the kishk is completely dry, use a mortar and pestle or food processor to grind it to a powder.

Store in an airtight container at room temperature up to 6 months.

Maydān's Shanklish
Cheese with Oil and Za'atar

Makes about 1¾ cups (300 g)

1 container (16 ounces / 455 g) labne

1 teaspoon fresh lemon juice

¾ teaspoon kosher salt

Extra-virgin olive oil, preferably Lebanese unfiltered, for serving

Za'atar, preferably Z&Z brand, for serving

Flatbread, for serving

Traditional Lebanese shanklish is made by curdling, straining, and fermenting labne until it is very dry and has even grown a bit of mold, which is an indication that it has achieved a tangy flavor that many people love. At Maydān we don't take it that far because we prefer a soft, spreadable shanklish that can be enjoyed during the meal like one of our dipping sauces (pages 29 to 39).

In a medium saucepan, combine the labne, lemon juice, salt, and ⅓ cup (75 ml) water. Whisk over medium heat until well blended and smooth. Continue to cook, stirring occasionally until the yogurt starts to separate.

Line a colander with six layers of fine cheesecloth. Put the colander into a pot or bowl big enough to let the liquid drip from the cheesecloth when poured in. Pour in the labne mixture and refrigerate for 24 hours.

Tie the ends of the top of the cheesecloth together and hang on a wooden spoon placed across the top of the bowl. Refrigerate for 2 days.

Remove the solid mixture from the cheesecloth and store in a covered container in the refrigerator up to 1 week.

To serve, transfer to a small serving dish. Use the back of a spoon to press a small divot in the surface of the shanklish. Pour in some olive oil and sprinkle over za'atar to garnish. Serve with bread.

Shankleesh
Spiced Cheese Balls

Makes about 1 dozen (2-inch / 5-cm) cheese balls

We primarily prepare soft, spreadable shanklish for the restaurant. But for special events we sometimes let a few batches ferment for a few more days. When it's dry enough to hold its shape when pressed together and the flavor has developed a bit more tang than when it's very fresh, we roll it into bite-size or slightly larger balls and roll them in spices. These balls are very pretty—and tasty! We put them into jars and cover with olive oil to preserve them longer.

Prepare Maydān's Shanklish, above. Let the mixture hang above the bowl until it is firm enough to hold its shape, 2 to 4 days longer.

Pour ½ cup (70 g) za'atar on a small plate. Have ready a 1-quart (960-ml) clean jar with a lid (see page 105).

Scoop up about 1 tablespoon of the yogurt and roll it into a ball in your hands (wet your hands if easier). Roll the ball lightly in the za'atar to coat evenly. Place the ball in the jar.

Continue with the remaining yogurt, adding more za'atar to the plate if necessary. When all of the yogurt is used, gently pour olive oil to cover into the jar.

Cover and store in the refrigerator for up to 6 months.

Fatayer bi Jibneh
Cheese Pies

Makes about 60 (2-inch / 5-cm)
fatayer; 10 to 12 servings

Dough for Sfeeha (page 136)

All-purpose flour, for the work surface

For the cheese filling and topping:
1 pound (455 g) Syrian cheese or low-moisture
mozzarella, grated by hand

½ cup (1 stick / 115 g) unsalted butter, melted,
plus more for baking sheets if using

3 tablespoons (30 g) white sesame seeds or
za'atar, preferably Z&Z brand, or as needed

No one in my family regularly made cheese-filled fatayer when I
was growing up, undoubtedly because of the lactose intolerance
that runs through us all. But when I finally tasted one on an
early trip to Lebanon, I quickly decided that they are worth the
discomfort. These little packages of savory melted cheese are
delightful. They will fly off the platter very quickly, so be sure to
sneak one for yourself before you put them out!

Make the dough, let it rise, and divide into 4 equal balls as for sfeeha.

Preheat the oven to 375°F (190°C). Grease two rimmed baking sheets,
or line them with parchment paper.

On a lightly floured work surface, working with one ball of dough at a time,
roll out the dough to ⅛ inch (3 mm) thick. Use a 3-inch (7.5 cm) cutter
to cut out rounds; set aside the dough scraps. Repeat with the remaining
dough. Combine the scraps, reroll, and cut out more rounds (you'll should
have about 60 rounds total). If at any point the dough springs back too
much when you roll it, or the cut rounds shrink excessively, cover the dough
with plastic wrap or a kitchen towel and let it rest for 10 to 20 minutes.

Spoon about 1 teaspoon grated cheese into the center of each round and
gently and gently pat it down so that there is a border of about 1 inch
(2.5 mm) all around. To shape the pies, lift and pinch together the dough
on two opposite sides (at 9 and 3 o'clock). Turn the pastry 90 degrees and
pinch together the two other opposite sides. You should have a pretty
square shape. If the dough is very sticky, dip your fingers in a little flour.

Repeat with the remaining dough rounds and cheese.

Place the pies 2 inches (5 cm) apart on the prepared baking sheets. Brush the
pies with melted butter and sprinkle lightly with sesame seeds or za'atar. Bake
until the bottoms are brown, 15 to 20 minutes. It's fine if some cheese melts
outside of the pies; you can just trim it off. Transfer to a wire rack to cool.

Serve hot, warm, or at room temperature. Store leftovers in a tightly
covered container at room temperature for 1 day or in the refrigerator for
up to 4 days.

Ayran
Yogurt Drink

Serves 2

2 cups (480 ml) ice cubes

2 cups (480 ml) labne

¼ cup (13 g) fresh mint leaves, chopped, plus sprigs for serving (optional)

¼ teaspoon kosher salt

This drink is ubiquitous at every kebab shop, man'ouche stand, and restaurant in Lebanon and throughout this part of the world. It's beloved and universal and consumed the same way as millions of American children drink milk with their dinners. It's too lactose-filled for me, unfortunately, but it's so refreshing and delightful that I'd drink it every day if I could.

In a blender combine the ice, labne, mint, if using, salt, and 1 cup (240 ml) water. Blend until smooth and frothy, adding more water if necessary to keep the mixture moving and make a thick but pourable drink.

Pour into two tall glasses, garnish with mint, if using, and serve cold.

8

Sweet Endings

Desserts

When I was a kid, dessert in our house was, in a word, fruit. I'm sure there were times that this really chafed, but today I'm grateful that I learned how to appreciate the natural sweetness of all kinds of fruit. That said, special occasions do call for special treats. Then, as now, that most often means phyllo-and-walnut-layered baklawa (which is an alternate spelling for baklava) and walnut-filled cookies called sambousek. And though I've added a few more to my repertoire since I was young, one thing that hasn't changed is how relatively restrained all of my favorite desserts are. The sweets I love most are based primarily on nuts and dried fruit and some phyllo and lots of sweet syrup flavored with rose or orange blossom water. I've heard friends in Lebanon joke that our desserts are light because we fill you up with so much food during the main meal that there's no room left for anything more at the end! In my experience, people always manage to find a little room for one or two of the items that follow.

Left: Coffee in Lebanon

IN THIS CHAPTER

Above: Roadside fruit stand, Oman

Right: Smoking shisha, Oman

Far right top: Pastry shop in the Baalbek souk

Far right bottom: Roasting coffee beans in Oman

كنافة بالجبن

K'nafe

Warm Cheese Dessert

Serves 8 to 12

½ cup (35 g) raw, unsalted pistachios

1 box (1 pound / 455 g) kataifi, thawed
(see Note)

1 cup (240 ml) clarified butter (recipe follows),
at room temperature

Softened butter, for the pie dish

3 cups (455 g) crumbled akkawi or low-moisture
mozzarella cheese (see Note)

2 teaspoons fresh lemon juice

2 teaspoons sugar

1 cup (240 ml) Rose Water Syrup (recipe
follows)

*Note: Kataifi, which is shredded phyllo dough,
and akkawi cheese are readily available at
Lebanese grocery stores.*

I first tasted this crisp, warm, melty cheese treat in southern Turkey in the town of Reyhanli where we spent several days cooking with refugee children from Syria (see page 139). I was surprised when I realized that the Lebanese have a sweet by the same name, but there it is a piece of sweetened bread, kind of like a challah roll, with cheese and honey inside. I have no idea why it's so different in Lebanon, and whether the difference has anything to do with the very heavy French influence in the country. Good thing we don't need the answers to enjoy any and all kinds of k'nafe. This one is especially good for anyone who loves salty-sweet and creamy-crunchy things.

Preheat the oven to 400°F (205°C).

Spread the pistachios on a rimmed baking sheet. Toast in the oven, stirring occasionally, until lightly browned and fragrant, 5 to 7 minutes. Immediately transfer the nuts to a plate to stop the cooking. Let cool, then finely grind in a food processor. Set aside. If making ahead, store in an airtight container for up to 3 days.

Lay the thawed bundle of kataifi on a cutting board and use a sharp knife to cut it into ½-inch (12 mm) pieces. Transfer to a large bowl. Pour the room temperature clarified butter into the bowl with the chopped kataifi. Using your hands, mix them together, working to coat each piece of kataifi with butter.

Spread the butter-coated kataifi in a thin layer on three or four rimmed sheet trays, depending on how many racks your oven has. Or toast the kataifi in batches; the key is to not layer the shredded phyllo too thickly to ensure that it browns evenly.

Bake, stirring and swapping the baking sheets between racks every 8 to 10 minutes, until golden brown, about 25 minutes. Remove from the oven and set aside. If finishing and serving right away, leave the oven on. If making ahead, let cool completely, then transfer the kataifi to a large, tightly covered container and store at room temperature for up to 1 week.

Leave the oven on, or if making the k'nafe at a later date, preheat the oven to 400°F (205°C). Rub a 9-inch (23 cm) pie dish with a thin layer of butter.

Spread half of the toasted kataifi on the bottom of the pie dish. Add the akkawi in an even layer and press the cheese down. Sprinkle with the lemon juice and sugar. Spread the remaining toasted kataifi on the top of the cheese.

Bake until the cheese starts to bubble, about 12 minutes. Immediately flip the k'nafe out onto a large serving plate. While hot, immediately pour over the rose water syrup and sprinkle with the ground toasted pistachios.

Slice; it's okay if the slices are a little messy. Serve hot.

[recipe continues]

Rose Water Syrup

Makes 3 cups (720 ml)

***

4 cups (800 g) sugar

1 tablespoon rose water

1 cardamom pod, crushed

***

In a large saucepan combine the sugar, rose water, cardamom pod, and 2 cups (480 ml) water.

Cook, stirring, over medium-high heat until the sugar is dissolved. Bring to a simmer and cook until the mixture is the consistency of light syrup (225°F [107°C]), about 40 minutes. Remove and discard the cardamom pod.

Keep warm until needed, or, if making ahead, store in an airtight container in the refrigerator up to 1 week. Gently reheat in a small saucepan before using.

Clarified Butter

Makes about 3½ cups (840 ml)

Regular butter is about 80 percent or so pure fat; the rest of the stick is water and milk proteins. Evaporating that water and removing the milk solids leaves pure butterfat, which has a much longer shelf life and higher smoke point than regular butter. The way I clarify butter, which is more like the method for making ghee, widely used in India and South Asia, is to simmer the butter long enough that the milk solids become lightly browned. It adds a nice nutty flavor to the butter. Note that butter like this can be used to fry food much more easily than regular butter; thanks to that higher smoke point, it won't burn as quickly as regular butter.

***

2 pounds (910 g) unsalted butter, cut into pieces

***

In a medium saucepan, melt the butter over low heat. You may stir at the beginning to move the butter around, but once it has melted, do not stir.

Skim off any foam that comes to the top. Once the foam is all removed, reduce the heat to very low and continue to cook until the butter is a golden color and the browned milk solids have fallen to the bottom of the pan.

Strain through a fine-mesh strainer lined with cheesecloth into a glass measuring cup. Let cool.

Store in a tightly covered container in the refrigerator for up to 8 months. Use for cooking, not for spreading on toast!

Fruit Plate with Orange Blossom Syrup

Serves 4

For the sugar syrup:
2 cups (400 g) sugar

1 teaspoon orange blossom water

8 ounces (225 g) fresh, ripe plums, pitted and sliced

8 ounces (225 g) fresh, ripe peaches, pitted and sliced

8 ounces (225 g) fresh, ripe apricots, pitted and sliced

8 ounces (225 g) fresh, ripe cherries, pitted

Torn fresh mint, for serving

It's very common in a restaurant in Lebanon to receive a lovely dish of fruit, sometimes in syrup, at the end of your meal, perhaps with the bill. When we visited my ancestral village, my cousins picked fruit straight off the trees outside their door, sliced and arranged them on ice, and poured sweet syrup over the whole thing. Honestly I have yet to see or taste an elaborate baked or frozen dessert that matches the beauty and flavor of a simple plate of fresh fruit in season gently lapped in orange blossom-laced syrup. It is key to use fruit in season, which in most of the U.S. means stone fruits and berries in summer (my favorite season and, I admit, my favorite iteration of this dish) and citrus fruits in winter; but what it means most of all is that when the fruit is truly the star of the show, as it is here, then the best result will come from using whatever is in season locally. What's available at farmers' markets is a good barometer of this, though I'm happy to say that more and more regular grocery stores will indicate when a fruit or vegetable is grown close by. Whatever fruit you choose, use about 2 to 3 pounds of it to serve four.

To make the syrup, in a large saucepan combine the sugar and 2 cups (480 ml) water. Bring to a boil over medium-high heat, stirring with a wooden spoon until the sugar is dissolved. Cover the pan and gently boil until slightly thickened, about 15 minutes. Remove from the heat and let cool.

Stir the orange blossom water into the cooled syrup. Chill until cold.

Arrange the fruit on a serving platter. Drizzle over the sugar syrup and garnish with torn mint and serve.

Ka'ak Sumsum
Sesame Cookies

Makes about 56 (2-inch / 5-cm) cookies

For the cookie dough:
1¼ cups (250 g) sugar

1 cup (240 ml) clarified butter (page 248)

5 teaspoons baking powder

2 large eggs

6 drops anise seed oil (see Note)

1 cup (240 ml) milk

6 cups (750 g) all-purpose flour

For the topping:
1 large egg

1 tablespoon milk

½ cup (75 g) white sesame seeds

1 drop anise seed oil (see Note)

Although I certainly remember eating a fair share of these classic, anise-laced Lebanese cookies on special occasions, I don't recall ever making them when I was a kid. We always picked them up at the Lebanese bakery when we were in Detroit. This is funny to me because they're so easy to make and such a pleasing, lightly sweetened treat to have with coffee or tea. In short, they're the perfect sweet for people who don't love sweets.

Preheat the oven to 350°F (175°C). Have ready 2 ungreased baking sheets.

To make the cookies, in a large bowl, stir together the sugar and butter. Add the baking powder, eggs, and anise seed oil and stir to combine. Gradually add the milk and flour alternately, stirring after each addition. Use your hands to knead the dough together well. Set aside.

For the topping, in a small dish, thoroughly beat the egg with the milk. In another dish put the sesame seeds. Add the drop of anise seed oil and stir with a fork to combine.

Pinch off a walnut-size piece of dough and roll it into a 4-inch (10 cm) long rope. Bring the ends together to form a circle.

Brush one side of the round with egg wash and dip lightly in the sesame seeds. Place seed side up on the ungreased baking sheets. Repeat with the remaining dough, egg, and sesame seeds, placing cookies 2 inches (5 cm) apart on the baking sheets.

Bake two sheets at a time until lightly browned, 15 to 20 minutes, switching and turning the baking sheets halfway through baking. Transfer cookies to a cooling rack to cool completely.

Store in a sealed container at room temperature for up to 1 week.

Note: Anise seed oil, extracted from the Pimpinella anisum *plant, adds a wonderful licorice flavor to baked goods. Buy anise seed oil online or in well-stocked grocery stores. It is quite strong, so use it sparingly. Note that star anise oil, extracted from the* Illicium verum *plant, has a similar flavor profile but is not the same.*

Ma'moul

Lebanese Date–Filled Butter Cookies

Makes about 2 dozen
(3-inch / 7.5-cm) cookies

For the dough:

1½ cups (3 sticks / 340 g) unsalted butter, at room temperature

¾ cup (150 g) sugar

1 tablespoon rose blossom water or orange, hazelnut, anise, or your favorite liqueur

2 large eggs

4¼ cups (530 g) all-purpose flour, plus more for the mold if needed

Vegetable oil for the mold if needed

For the date filling:

1 pound (455 g) pitted soft dates, coarsely chopped or snipped with scissors (see Note)

2 tablespoons unsalted butter, melted

½ cup (65 g) confectioners' sugar, for finishing

Equipment: Ma'moul mold (easy to order online)

A ma'moul is a buttery cookie surrounding a sweet date filling. Shaped using a special mold, it is a popular addition to holiday dessert tables throughout the region. Ma'moul are often made with some semolina, which gives the cookie a pleasing crumbly texture; in my family, though, we made ma'moul using only flour, which results in a very tender cookie that I love.

To prepare the dough, in an electric stand mixer fitted with the paddle attachment, beat the butter on medium speed until lightened in color and texture, 3 to 5 minutes.

Scrape down the sides of the bowl and add the sugar and rose water. Mix until thoroughly combined, scraping down the sides of the bowl. Add the eggs and beat until well blended.

Gradually add the flour, beating in with a mixer at first, then kneading by hand, until all ingredients are completely blended. Press the dough into a flat disk, wrap it in plastic wrap, and refrigerate for 30 minutes.

Meanwhile, to prepare the date filling, place the dates and melted butter in a food processor. Process until finely chopped. Scoop up 1 tablespoon of the date mixture at a time and roll into 1¼-inch (3.2 cm) balls. Set aside.

Preheat the oven to 375°F (190°C). Line a baking sheet with parchment.

Pull off a walnut-size piece of dough and pat it in a 3-inch (7.5 cm) round. Place a date ball in the middle of it; close the round and place it in a 2½- to 3-inch (6 to 7.5 cm) ma'moul mold. Press lightly to imprint the design.

Invert the mold and rap it firmly on the table to remove the pressed cookie. It may help to rap it once on either side of the mold as well. Repeat with the remaining date balls and cookie dough. Though these cookies must be made one at a time, once you get the hang of the process, it will go very quickly.

Note that if the dough is sticking to the mold, lightly oiling with vegetable oil and/or flouring the mold between each cookie can help. If the dough is very soft, return it to the refrigerator for a few minutes. Remember that you can always remove the dough from the mold, again roll it into a ball between your hands, and reshape it in the mold.

Place the cookies 2 inches (5 cm) apart on the lined baking sheet and bake one sheet at a time until cookies are lightly browned on the bottom, 15 to 20 minutes.

Cool on the baking sheet for 5 minutes, then transfer the cookies to cooling racks to cool completely.

Sprinkle with confectioners' sugar before serving. Store the ma'moul in an airtight container at room temperature up to 2 weeks.

Note: Lightly coat the blade of the knife or scissors with neutral vegetable oil if the dates are sticking.

Left: Ka'ak Sumsum (page 250) and Ma'moul (this page) with Halwa (page 263)

Sambousek
Walnut–Filled Half–Moon Cookies

Makes 5 to 6 dozen sambousek

For the dough:
4½ cups (563 g) all-purpose flour, plus more for the work surface

2½ teaspoons ground anise seed

2 teaspoons mahlab (ground cherry pits, see Note)

1 cup (2 sticks / 225 g) salted butter

¾ to 1 cup (180 to 240 ml) milk

¼ cup (60 ml) vegetable oil

¼ teaspoon active dry yeast

For the syrup:
2 cups (400 g) sugar

2¼ teaspoons fresh lemon juice

1½ teaspoons orange flower water

For the filling:
1 pound (455 g) walnuts, coarsely ground in a food processor

1 cup (200 g) sugar

1 tablespoon orange blossom water

These are my most favorite cookies. When I was growing up, a few times a year, always in advance of a major event such as a wedding or holiday, my aunts would swoop down on us for a full day or two, and they'd commandeer our kitchen and dining room with their baking assembly line. Everyone was assigned a task, whether it was mixing dough, rolling and cutting, filling, crimping, or baking and dipping. During their studious labor, literally hundreds of these tender walnut hand pies would be filled, formed, baked, and dipped while still warm in fragrant sugar syrup laced with orange flower water. This family production is what my cousins call a "sambousek bee," after the gatherings of people (mostly women, if we're being honest) who come together to sew lots of useful items and then swap them. In my child's mind, celebrations became inexorably linked to teeming platters of sambousek, an association that stays with me. They only grow tastier with time so feel free to prepare them several days before you plan to serve them.

To make the dough, in a large bowl, whisk together the flour, anise, and mahlab. Set aside.

In a large saucepan, melt the butter. Add ¾ cup (180 ml) milk and the oil and heat to lukewarm (about 110°F [45°C]). Stir in the yeast.

Make a hole in the center of the flour and pour in the milk mixture. Using a spatula and then your hands, blend until there is no more dry flour and the dough is smooth; if the dough is very dry, add the remaining milk 1 tablespoon at a time. Cover the bowl with plastic wrap and let stand at room temperature for 1 hour.

Knead the dough, cover the bowl with plastic wrap, and let stand in a warm place for 30 minutes. Meanwhile, make the syrup and filling.

To make the syrup, in a medium saucepan combine the sugar, lemon juice, and 1 cup (240 ml) water. Bring to a boil over medium-high heat, stirring with a wooden spoon until the sugar is dissolved. Cover the pan and gently boil until the syrup thickens very slightly, 10 to 15 minutes. Remove from the heat and let cool.

Stir the orange blossom water into the cooled syrup. Chill until cold.

To make the filling, place the walnuts, sugar, and orange blossom water in a medium bowl. Using your hands, mix until well blended and there are no lumps. Set aside.

Have ready several ungreased or parchment-lined baking sheets.

Divide the dough into 4 pieces and shape into rounds. Cover with a kitchen towel to keep them from drying out. Working with one round at a time, on a lightly floured surface, roll out the dough to ⅛ inch (3 mm) thick. Using the

rim of a rocks glass (like we always do) or a roughly 3-inch (7.5 cm) round cookie or biscuit cutter, cut the dough into rounds.

Place 1 teaspoon walnut filling in the center of the round. Fold over to enclose the filling and form a half-moon shape; pinch the edges together to seal.

Place the cookies on the baking sheets up to 1 inch (2.5 cm) apart; they won't rise very much. Repeat with the remaining dough (including scraps, which you can reroll) and filling. Cover both the unused dough and the baking sheets of filled unbaked cookies to keep both from drying out.

When ready to bake, arrange oven racks in the center and top of the oven and preheat the oven to 375°F (190°C).

Bake one sheet at a time on the center rack until the bottoms of the cookies are golden brown, about 12 minutes, then transfer the pan to the top rack and bake until the tops are lightly browned, about 5 minutes.

Remove from the oven and dip the whole, still-warm cookies in the syrup. Scoop them out of the syrup using a fork so the excess syrup can easily pour off the cookies and place on a cooling rack until completely cooled. (Store any remaining filling or syrup in airtight containers in the refrigerator for up to 6 months)

Store the sambousek in an airtight container at room temperature up to 2 weeks (they get better with time). For longer storage, place layers of parchment or wax paper between them. Cover tightly and freeze up to 6 months. Let stand in a single layer, unwrapped, at room temperature, to defrost.

Note: Ground mahlab, which adds a very specific and delightful warm, nutty aroma and flavor to these cookies, is available in Lebanese grocery stores and is also easy to find online.

Aunt Gracie's Harist Il Louz

Cream of Wheat Cake

Makes 24 (2-inch / 5-cm) squares

For the syrup:

2 cups (400 g) sugar

Juice of ½ lemon

1 teaspoon orange blossom water

For the pudding squares:

Vegetable oil, for spraying the baking pan, and for the knife (optional)

4 cups (960 ml) milk

2 cups (360 g) Cream of Wheat

1¾ cups (350 g) sugar

1 cup (2 sticks / 225 g) salted butter

24 whole blanched almonds or about ½ cup (55 g) slivered almonds, for garnish

This is the dessert that I most associate with my childhood. Our aunt Gracie brought it whenever she visited, and I loved it so much that we asked her for the recipe. Eventually I took to baking it myself whenever I could, making it one of the very few things that I made as a young person that wasn't directly from my mom or dad's repertoire. In fact, it wasn't even a family recipe. Though we regarded Gracie as one of our many aunties, my cousin Rachel and I didn't realize until high school that she was actually a very dear friend of our great-aunt Babe, not a blood relative. It cracks me up and warms my heart to think about how as children we never questioned that everyone who was at all of our holiday gatherings was family.

To make the syrup, in a medium saucepan combine the sugar with 2 cups (480 ml) water. Bring to a simmer over medium heat. Stir to ensure the sugar is dissolved. Bring to a boil and add the lemon juice. Simmer for 20 minutes. Remove the pan from the heat, stir in the orange blossom water, and set aside to cool completely. Refrigerate until cold.

Preheat the oven to 375°F (190°C). Spray a 9 by 12-inch (23 by 30.5 cm) baking pan with oil.

To make the pudding squares, in a large saucepan stir together the milk, Cream of Wheat, sugar, and butter. Cook over medium-low heat, stirring constantly, until the mixture comes away from the sides of the pan, about 15 minutes; it will be thick and it will thicken before it comes away from the sides of the pan.

Scrape the mixture into the prepared pan and use a rubber or silicone spatula to make an even layer. Use a sharp knife to cut 2 inch (5 cm) squares (rubbing vegetable oil on the knife can help prevent sticking). Put a whole almond or a few slivered almonds in the center of each square and press very gently so they stick.

Bake until lightly browned, 50 minutes to 1 hour, and up to 10 minutes longer for a browner top.

Remove from the oven and recut the squares. Spoon the cold syrup around the outer edges and all the cut edges; don't add more syrup than the harist can absorb—you may not use all of the syrup.

Let cool completely in the pan. Store in an airtight container at room temperature up to 2 weeks.

Qatayef with Ashtaliyeh
Sweet Pancakes with Cream Pudding

Makes about 40 filled pancakes

For the ashta:

3 cups (720 ml) milk

½ cup (65 g) cornstarch

¼ cup (50 g) sugar

1 tablespoon rose water

1 tablespoon orange blossom water

For the syrup:

2½ cups (500 g) sugar

Juice of ½ lemon

2 teaspoons rose water

2 teaspoons orange blossom water

For the pancakes:

2½ cups (310 g) all-purpose flour

2 teaspoons baking powder

½ cup (240 ml) lukewarm water
(110°F [45°C])

1 tablespoon sugar

1 teaspoon active dry yeast

2 cups (480 ml) milk

For finishing:

⅓ cup (45 g) raw, unsalted pistachios,
coarsely chopped

Food-safe dried rose petals (optional)

For this treat, small, yeasted pancakes cooked on only one side are rolled into a cone and filled with a beautifully light cream laced with rose and orange blossom waters. The cream ends of the cones are dipped in crushed pistachios and then the whole platter of them or individual servings are drizzled with a delicate syrup that is also flavored with rose and orange blossom waters. These delights are very common in the region.

To make the ashta, in a glass measuring cup or small bowl, combine 1½ cups (360 ml) of the milk with the cornstarch and whisk until smooth. Set the slurry aside.

In a large saucepan, combine the remaining 1½ cups (360 ml) milk with the sugar and heat over medium heat until the sugar is dissolved, stirring occasionally. Continue to heat until the milk begins to bubble. Whisk in the cornstarch slurry and continue to whisk until the mixture is very thick, 2 to 4 minutes. Remove the pan from the heat and whisk in the rose and orange blossom waters.

Transfer the ashta to a heat-proof bowl and press a piece of plastic wrap flush against the surface, to prevent a skin from forming. Set aside to cool, then refrigerate until cold.

To make the syrup, in a medium saucepan, combine the sugar and 1¼ cups (300 ml) water. Bring to a boil over medium heat, stirring occasionally. Add the lemon juice, and reduce the heat to boil gently until slightly thickened, about 5 minutes.

Remove the pan from the heat and stir in the rose and orange blossom waters. Let cool completely. The syrup can be stored in an airtight container in the refrigerator for up to 1 week.

To make the pancakes, in a large bowl, whisk together the flour and baking powder. In a separate large bowl, whisk together the water, sugar, and yeast. Let stand until foamy, about 10 minutes. Whisk the milk into the water mixture. Slowly add the liquid ingredients into the flour, whisking until smooth.

Let stand at room temperature for 1 hour. After this hour, if not using the batter at once, refrigerate until ready to cook the pancakes.

When ready to cook the pancakes, heat a nonstick skillet over medium to medium-high heat until hot and set a cooling rack on a baking sheet next to the stove. For each pancake, add about 1½ tablespoons batter to the pan to form a 3½-inch (9-cm) circle. You can cook more than one at a time; just don't crowd the pan. Bubbles will appear almost at once on the top of the pancakes; if they do not, increase the heat. Cook until the bubbles have popped, the surface is dry, and the bottom is lightly golden. Transfer them to the cooling rack to cool slightly; do not flip the pancakes over and cook the other side!

It's fine if your first few pancakes are not very shapely; it can take a few tries to get the pan to the correct temperature and to get a feel for cooking them. If the pancakes are spreading too quickly and are misshapen, whisk in more flour a couple of teaspoons at a time; if they aren't bubbling much and you're sure your pan is hot enough, whisk in more milk a couple of teaspoons at a time.

When the pancakes are still warm but cool enough to handle, shape them into a cone shape: Hold one pancake with the uncooked side facing up. Fold it loosely in half and starting at one of the two folded ends, press together the two open edges about two-thirds of the way up the side, leaving an opening at the top.

Use the remaining batter to cook the pancakes and shape them into cones. Let cool for a few minutes before assembling.

To assemble, place the pistachios in a shallow dish. Remove the ashta from the refrigerator; it will be very thick. Whisk it vigorously until smooth. Transfer the cream to a pastry bag fitted with a large round tip or use a disposable pastry bag and snip off the end after the bag is filled.

Pipe the cream into a cone, filling it pretty generously. Dip the exposed cream into the pistachios and arrange the assembled qatayef on a plate. Continue with the remaining pancakes, cream, and pistachios. Scatter some rose petals on top, if desired. Serve with the syrup for drizzling.

These are best the day they are made. Store leftovers in an airtight container in the refrigerator for up to 2 days.

Baklawa

Makes about 80 (1½-inch / 4-cm) pieces

For the filling:

2 pounds (910 g) shelled walnuts, ground medium-fine in a food processor

¾ cup (150 g) sugar

2 to 3 tablespoons orange blossom water

For the syrup (see Notes):

1½ cups (300 g) sugar

Juice of ½ lemon

3 tablespoons orange blossom water

2 pounds (32 ounces / 910 g) phyllo dough, thawed (see Notes)

2 pounds (910 g) salted butter, clarified (see page 248 and Notes)

When I was in college, I was the president of the Amnesty International chapter at my university and a lovely art professor was the dedicated faculty advisor to our little group (we had all of about five members). For a fundraiser around the holidays one year, we decided we would make small pottery plates and sell them. We set up outside the cafeteria where there was a very regular stream of students coming in and out. Right next to the plates we placed a petition to stop the Iraq war, and our goal was to get their signatures and their money. Even then, when I saw a plate, I decided it must be filled, and I enlisted my mom to help me make a bunch of baklawa for a little extra incentive. It was definitely a sign of things to come in my life, though the student body at Ohio Northern was generally more conservative than me, and most who passed by were as suspicious of my baklawa as they were of my petition. How foolish they were to shun the virtues of this golden baked phyllo pastry filled with buttery ground nuts and bathed in fragrant syrup. Even though I'll choose salty over sweet most days of the week, I always make an exception for my mom's baklawa.

In Lebanon, baklawa is filled with walnuts instead of pistachios only during Ramadan. Perhaps this is because walnuts are especially filling, which is important when adults eat only after sundown for an entire month. In my family, however, we always use walnuts. This generous recipe makes enough for a crowd and then some; but don't hesitate to make this if you're serving a smaller group; leftovers keep beautifully for weeks. It's important to cut the baklawa all the way through before you bake it; you won't be able to do it afterwards without crushing the pastry, and those cuts allow the syrup to soak all the way through every piece, which is key to baklawa's divine flavor and texture.

To make the filling, in a large bowl combine the walnuts, sugar, and orange blossom water and use your hands to rub it all together until well mixed with no lumps. Set aside.

To make the syrup, in a medium saucepan, combine the sugar and 3 cups (720 ml) water. Bring to a boil over medium heat, then boil gently for 15 minutes. Add the lemon juice and cook another 5 minutes. Remove the pan from the heat and stir in the orange blossom water. Let cool completely, then chill until cold.

Arrange a rack in the middle of the oven and preheat the oven to 400°F (205°C). Have ready a 17 by 12 by 1½-inch (43 by 30.5 by 4 cm) baking pan. Trim the phyllo dough if necessary to fit the pan. Brush the bottom and sides of the pan with a thin layer of butter.

[recipe continues]

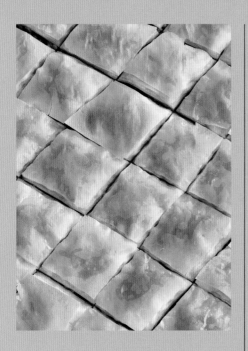

While working with phyllo, make sure to keep the dough that you're pulling from covered with plastic wrap and a kitchen towel so that it won't dry out.

Place one sheet of phyllo on the bottom of the pan and lightly brush butter over the entire sheet. Repeat with each layer, buttering each layer until 1 pound (455 g) of phyllo is used; do not butter the last sheet.

Place the nut mixture on top and use your hands to spread it into an even layer and pat it down lightly.

Using the other pound of phyllo, place a sheet on top of the nuts and lightly brush it with butter. Continue in the same manner as before with the second pound of dough, making sure each layer is lightly buttered.

Cut the baklawa into squares or diamonds before baking. To cut it into diamonds, starting at the short side of the pan, score the middle of the pastry. From that point score at intervals of two finger widths or approximately 1 inch (2.5 cm). You should have 8 rows marked. Use a very sharp knife to cut down the length of each scored line, slicing all the way through all the layers of dough.

Turn the pan 90 degrees and score diagonally at even intervals across all the rows; you will have 80 to 90 pieces. Use your knife to cut all the way through all the layers.

Bake the baklawa for 15 minutes. Turn the oven temperature down to 325°F (165°C) and bake until the top layer is flaky and a light golden brown, about 45 minutes.

Remove the baklawa from the oven, and while it is still hot, pour the syrup all over the surface of the pastry, first going down the sides and then continuing row by row, covering the full width and length of the baklawa.

Let cool completely in the pan. You may serve directly from the pan. Cover the pan or transfer to an airtight container and store at room temperature for up to 2 weeks.

Notes: Have syrup and clarified butter prepared at least one day ahead. If you have the option, buy the thinnest phyllo you can. If there are numbers on the boxes, buy the one marked "#4 thin."

Halwa

Tahini Cocktail

Makes 1 cocktail and enough syrup
for 16 cocktails

For the tahini syrup:
1 cup (240 ml) tahini (sesame seed paste),
preferably Beirut brand, stirred until smooth
before measuring

1 cup (240 ml) hot water

¾ cup (150 g) sugar

¾ teaspoon kosher salt

¼ teaspoon vanilla extract

¼ teaspoon orange blossom water

For one cocktail:
Ice, for mixing

1½ ounces (45 ml) tequila, such as Pueblo
Viejo Reposado

1 ounce (30 ml) tahini syrup

½ ounce (15 ml) orange liqueur, such as Combier

½ ounce (15 ml) fresh lime juice

Ground pistachios, for garnish

This cocktail, created by Nari Kim, an opening bartender at Maydān, somehow manages to be creamy without any cream or dairy at all. It has just the right amount of sweetness—not too much, not too little—to make it the perfect partner to sip with any of the desserts in this chapter (as you can see on page 252). Or, if you truly can't imagine eating one more thing, this drink can easily stand on its own as a lovely sweet ending.

To make the tahini syrup, place the tahini, hot water, sugar, salt, vanilla, and orange blossom water in a blender. Blend until smooth. Store in a covered container in the refrigerator for up to 1 week.

To make a cocktail, fill a cocktail shaker with ice.

Pour into the shaker the tequila, tahini syrup, orange liqueur, and lime juice. Close the shaker and shake vigorously until the outside of the shaker is uncomfortably cold.

Strain into a coupe glass and garnish with a sprinkle of ground pistachios.

Resources

BATCH 13
batch13wines.com
A great wine and spirits shop in Washington, DC, with a huge selection of Georgian wines.

BEIT DOUMA
hotelibanais.com/travel/guesthouses/beit-douma
In the village of Douma, Lebanon, one of the most beautiful, restful inns anywhere.

BURLAP AND BARREL
burlapandbarrel.com
Everything they have is good, including their ground sumac and ground black lime.

CHANI NICHOLAS
chani.com
For reading the stars.

EL CAMINO TRAVEL
elcamino.travel
For incredible experiences all over the world.

GO THERE WINES
gotherewines.com
My social-impact wine company.

J.Q. DICKINSON
jqdsalt.com
For phenomenal West Virginian salt.

KUZEH POTTERY
kuzehpottery.com
The female-owned business behind the beautiful bowls and plates at Maydān.

LAITERIE HADWANE
hadwan.weebly.com/blog
A delightful dairy and provisions shop in the town of Mreijat, in Lebanon's Beqaa region.

MAYDĀN, COMPASS ROSE, KIRBY CLUB, and MEDINA
maydandc.com
compassrosedc.com
kirbyclub.com
medinadc.com
So I can feed you like family in Washington, DC, and Northern Virginia.

MAYDĀN LA
4301 West Jefferson Boulevard, Los Angeles, CA 90016
Like the original with some West Coast touches; coming to the West Adams neighborhood in spring 2024.

SAHADI'S
sahadis.com
If you find yourself in Brooklyn, stop in here for almost any ingredient you need.

SANTA MONICA FARMERS MARKET
santamonica.gov/places/farmers-markets/downtown-farmers-market
If you're in or near Santa Monica on a Wednesday or Saturday, this is the place to come for beautiful produce.

SUPRA
supradc.com
For incredible Georgian food in Washington, DC.

TASTE LEBANON
facebook.com/tastelebanon
My friend Bethany's company organizes fabulous culinary tours in Lebanon.

TIGER BAKERY & DELI
tigerbakery.com
My childhood bakery; stop by if you're in Toledo!

WEST LA INTERNATIONAL MARKET
westlainternationalmarket.com
This is where I go when I'm cooking at home in LA and I run out of those pantry staples.

Z&Z
zandzdc.com
A family-owned bakery in suburban DC with the best za'atar in America.

ZINGERMAN'S
zingermans.com
Fantastic ingredients and prepared foods, and also fun salts.

Left: Trying to figure out which jar won't leak in my suitcase

Above: Omani spice blend

Index

Acknowledgments

This book is dedicated to all the women in my family and across the globe who have taught me a recipe, a technique, shown me enormous hospitality, or shared a family secret.

Not only would I not be where I am today without them, but this book would not be in your hands right now if it wasn't for my family. Thank you, Aunt Jan, Aunt Joan, Aunt Jen, Uncle Buddy, and cousin Rachel. And all the cousins and relatives who helped with recipes. They are the beautiful spirits who overcame their fear of measuring cups and spoons to help us record the dishes they have made from their hearts for so, so many years. With a limited amount of arguing, they helped to record the recipes handed down to them by their grandmothers, to my grandmother, and now to my brothers, cousins, and me. My brothers and sisters-in-law, thank you for your undying patience with my work and your loving support of all my crazy ideas. Albert, Maggie, Peter, Becca, Joey, and Kris, sorry for all the dinners when I was on the phone and for only taking you out to eat at one of my restaurants.

Mom and Dad. Thank you for teaching me to love and respect food. Thank you for forcing me to learn that being different was always the way to go, even when it's hard. That food would be the way we explain who we are and why we're proud of it. Mom, your unrelenting work ethic and devotion to us kids is rare and special and molded us into some real, beautiful characters. It's true, the food doesn't taste good unless you cook with love in your heart. Thanks, Dad, for the decades of subscribing to *Gourmet* magazine and buying all the cookbooks that taught me about how to follow a recipe and about far-away worlds.

Marah. My dear and benevolent coauthor. We laugh at how we finished this book very different than the people who started it. We persevered through a pandemic to collaborate on recipes that we couldn't cook together as we couldn't be in the same room for most of the writing of this book. Somewhere in the middle recipe sessions turned to therapy sessions and we have weathered more than one meltdown together. I am eternally grateful for you in every possible way. How do you trust someone to be your voice? I'm so glad Marah accepted my request that she help me put so many thoughts, ideas, memories, musings, peculiarities, and all-assorted melee into beautiful prose.

Thank you to the chefs who shared their time and their own special dishes with me for this book, especially Darnell, Omar, and John Paul. Thank you to Sameen and Victoria and Bella and Mamuka and Lina and Lena. Thank you, Karam Foundation, for a week of learning and unlearning and appreciation for what it is to overcome great hardship and carry your culture with you when the world took away everything else away from you.

Thank you, Bethany and Eddie, for leading me on my journey to connect to my ancestral homeland. Thank you for understanding that food and wine can connect us across generations and miles. You are amazing teachers and torchbearers of a rich and beautiful culture. Many thanks to Felicia for helping us create an amazing culinary trip through Oman and for writing an amazing cookbook that inspired us to travel there.

Thank you, Mariana, Caroline, Maeve, and the whole production team who worked like crazy before the holidays to get our photos taken in time.

The indomitable Jen. Thank you for seeing me exactly as I am and somehow showing the world via your beautiful photos. I trust you like none other even if you didn't give me mezcal and music to get through a shoot.

Mike, you indulge my many wild ideas and support the visions and dreams that many wouldn't trust could turn into beautiful as well as successful things. Thank you for trusting me and believing in me. Andy, thank you for saying, "Let me know when you're ready to do the next one." Look where we went with that! Thank you for trusting me even when you didn't really understand how the space was ever going to come together.

David, Sarah, Laura, and Diane, thank you for taking a chance on a first-time author from Washington, DC. Thank you, Joe, for the introduction, and Maddy, who told me I could do this.

Thank you, Maydān, and the teams past and present. Thank you, Christina, Drew, and Jessie, especially for your hand modeling and traveling with me, literally and figuratively.

David Greene. You taught me that anything is possible and there is no ocean wide enough and no mountain tall enough nor any train journey long enough that we can't attempt to cross or climb or ride together. Your insane love of adventure is contagious and I'm so glad I caught it from you so very long ago. I'm sorry I'm still bad with maps, but I vow to always have snacks in my bag for us. I write this with the advance thanks for the next adventure that I know is right around the corner.

To the migrants and the refugees and those fighting in this region to preserve their cultures and their homes through food, even after their homes and countries have been stolen from them. There are so few easy days. I can't thank you enough for the days and nights you've given me to learn from you and share your gifts with the world.

Editor: Laura Dozier
Design Manager: Danielle Youngsmith
Managing Editor: Glenn Ramirez
Production Manager: Kathleen Gaffney

Book design by Diane Shaw

Library of Congress Control Number: 2023932419

ISBN: 978-1-4197-6313-7
eISBN: 978-1-64700-746-1

Printed and bound in China
10 9 8 7 6 5 4 3 2 1

ABRAMS The Art of Books
195 Broadway, New York, NY 10007
abramsbooks.com

Rose Previte is the owner of
Washington, DC's acclaimed restaurants
Compass Rose, Maydān, Kirby Club, and Medina.
She is also the cofounder of Go There Wines, a social-impact
wine company. Raised in a food-loving Sicilian-Lebanese family in Ohio,
Rose started working in food in her mother's restaurant and Lebanese
catering business. Her first restaurant was inspired by spending nearly
three years traveling to more than thirty countries, all while
she lived in Russia with her husband, David Greene, posted there
as the correspondent for NPR. She lives a bicoastal life
between Los Angeles and Washington, DC.

Marah Stets is a *New York Times* bestselling writer.
She lives in the Washington, DC, area
with her family and dogs.